Methodological Pluralism
& Qualitative Family Research

Jane F. Gilgun, Ph.D

University of Minnesota,

Twin Cities, USA

April 9, 1997

Published as Gilgun, Jane F. (1999). Methodological pluralism and qualitative family research. In Suzanne K. Steinmetz, Marvin B. Sussman, and Gary W. Peterson (Eds.), *Handbook of Marriage and the Family* (2nd ed.) (pp. 219-261). New York: Plenum. The author thanks reviewers Katherine Allen, Kerry Daly, and one anonymous reviewer for their helpful comments and editors Sue Steinmetz, Marv Sussman, and Gary "Pete" Peterson for cheering me on and for offering valuable suggestions.

Methodological Pluralism & Qualitative Family Research
by Jane Gilgun
101 pages

ISBN-13: 978-1499716191
ISBN-10: 1499716192

1. research methods 2. methodology 3. Qualitative research
4. Chicago School of Sociology 5. Analytic induction
6. Phenomenological research 7. Case study research

Also by Jane Gilgun

Books

Chicago School Traditions: Deductive Qualitative Analysis & Grounded Theory
Child Sexual Abuse: From Harsh Realities to Hope
Children with Serious Conduct Issues
I Want to Show You: Poems
On Being a Sh*t: Unkind Deeds & Cover-Ups in Everyday Life
The NEATS: A Child & Family Assessment

Children's Books

Busjacked!
Daddy Loves Me
Emma and her Forever Person
Five Little Cygnets Cross the Bundoran Road
Lemons or Lemonade: An Anger Workbook for Kids
Lemons or Lemonade: An Anger Workbook for Teens
Salamander: A Story of Two Boys
The King's Toast
The Little Pig Who Didn't go to Market
Turtle Night at Playa Grande
Will the Soccer Star

Short Pieces

An Intellectual History of Grounded Theory
Attachment & Child Development
Coding in Deductive Qualitative Research
Detecting the Potential for Violence
Executive Function & Self-Regulation in Children
Family Incest Treatment & Professional Treatment for Abusers
Neurobiology, Trauma, & Child Development
Reflexivity & Qualitative Research
Talking to Children Who Have Been Sexually Abused
The Sex Education of Children
Two Boys, Similar Backgrounds: One Goes to Prison & One Does Not: Why?
What Sexual Abuse Means to Child Survivors
What Sexual Abuse Means to Abusers
What Child Sexual Abuse Means to Girl & Women Perpetrators

Manuals

Readiness to Adopt Children with Specials Needs
CASPARS: Tools for Assessing Client Strengths & Risks

3

Methodological Pluralism
and Qualitative Family Research

Methodological pluralism is a hallmark of contemporary research on families. Such pluralism is not likely to go away because it is firmly embedded in tradition and in the methodological transformations current in the social and human sciences. Practicing in a wide array of disciplines, family scholars are being swept up in--and helping to create--the exciting possibilities these transformations present. Such possibilities are so recent that the words of LaRossa and Reitzes (1993), written not long ago, though compelling, soon will be outdated. They wrote, "family research is for the most part dominated by relatively static models and methodologies" (p. 158), an observation other family scholars have articulated (e.g., Osmond, 1987; Thomas & Wilcox, 1987). The exploration of methodological stasis in family research will provide a context in which to interpret the state of contemporary qualitative family research methods. As I will show, methodological stasis is a relatively recent phenomena. Research on families stands on a tradition of methodological pluralism.

In the not so distant past in most training institutions and funding agencies, one approach to research was taken for granted and not named. Students had virtually no choice as to the philosophy of science to which they were exposed and the kinds of research that professors and others in authority expected them to do. Researchers seeking funding, publication, and tenure were restricted in how they could approach research questions. The dominance of a particular type of research was so entrenched that those who taught it, wrote about it, and practiced it rarely reflected on this hegemony and its impact. There was a single, hallowed term for this type of research: science. A positivistic style of doing science, the general approach was based on the measurement of observables and on deduction; that is, on theories that already had been created. To some extent, this positivistic, deductive hegemony still exists. Many young scholars wait until after they attain tenure before they embark upon the great methodological adventures offered by qualitative approaches to studies of families. These pursuits are also part of science, but a form of science usually based on approaches that are inductive and interpretive in nature. In these interpretive versions of science, unobservables, such as experience, perceptions, and memories, are of interest, and the generation of new understandings, concepts, and theories are goals.

What accounts for the creation of the hegemony of positivistic, deductive science and what accounts for its breaking apart is not clear. One term, however, sums up what is happening: postmodernism. (See Doherty, this volume, for an extended discussion of postmodernism.) More than anything else, a sense that researchers can say and do whatever they want characterizes postmodernism in social and human sciences. The only constraint on absolute freedom that I see in contemporary research is self-imposed and perhaps based on common-sense; that is, if I want to communicate with others, I have to use language and approaches that others can understand, or, if my approaches and my language are not intelligible to my audiences of interest, I must explain in terms that are familiar. In my teaching and research, I have found, however, that even the clearest exposition possible of a research project that departs from positivistic, deductive approaches may not be well understood because the ideas behind the project are unfamiliar.

The task of writing about qualitative family research in today's postmodern contexts involves the impossible task of imposing order on the near-chaos that characterizes contemporary research on families. A kaleidoscope is a metaphor that helps me think about what is happening at the moment. Turn it just a bit, and new visions open up. Keep turning and additional forms appear. Each turn creates new possibilities, representing the yet unexplored vistas of qualitative family research.

Methods as a Starting Point

Methods as a starting point is an unusual approach in family scholarship. Other appraisals of the state of the scholarship, particularly since the 1950s, have focused almost exclusively on theory and sometimes on methodologies. Sadly, appraisal after appraisal is characterized by despair over the state of family theory (Adams, 1988; Lavee & Dollahite, 1991; Larzarlee & Klein, 1987; Nye, 1988; Osmond, 1987; Thomas & Wilcox, 1987). When scholars discuss methodologies that are promising in terms of generating theory, they stop short of making links to the procedures that will actualize methodological principles. This, of course, is understandable because of the challenges inherent in in-depth methodological analyses. Nonetheless, somehow we as a scholarly community need to encourage each other to push ourselves toward the actualization that methodologies encourage. For example, in an exemplary review of radical-critical theories, Osmond critiqued positivism in family studies and called for research methods that are "true to the nature of the phenomena being studied" (p. 121). Although she provided a multi-layered and potentially generative basis for the development of research procedures that could lead the field into a post-positivistic future, she did not suggest methods that might do so.

Lazerlee and Klein (1987) also were concerned with methods that fit family research and would help generate theory. In their exploration of the possibilities, they discussed qualitative methods, the one set of methods that I believe has the most promise of generating theory. Unfortunately, they did not do an in-depth analysis, assuming perhaps that other scholars will pick up on this important insight. Books that might have greatly advanced the development of family theory include Glaser's (1978) neglected classic, *Theoretical Sensitivity*, whose purpose is to offer "a rigorous, orderly guide to theory development" (p. 2) and Glaser and Strauss's (1967) *The Discovery of Grounded Theory*. Both volumes lay out in clear language methods and methodologies of systematically generating theory from either qualitative or quantitative data.

In this chapter, I want to bring attention to the potential significance of qualitative methods for advancing family theory and for deepening and broadening our understandings of the often hidden and private realms of meaning related to experiences of family life. Though my experience suggests that starting with methods will be an improvement over a focus on theory and methodologies, I am not certain. This essay will explore the possibilities.

The proof of the value of qualitative methods is in their products. The necessity of showing the products of qualitative research is pressing. Though some of the classic studies of families are based on qualitative methods, contemporary qualitative researchers must make their cases anew that this style of research has something important to offer, such as adding to knowledge and understanding and in promoting the common good. Otherwise, the research community, policy makers, program planners, practitioners, journal editors, and funders will not take qualitative research seriously. More than 130 years ago, LePlay (1866) made a similar point when he said that social scientists justify their methods by the results.

Principles Guiding This Chapter

I have been deeply challenged personally and intellectually as I attempt to understand and do qualitative family research. In my roles as professor, researcher, and editor of other scholars' qualitative family research (e.g., Gilgun & Sussman, 1996; Gilgun, Daly, & Handel, 1992) I have observed the grit and intellect that other scholars have displayed as they, too, struggle to learn how to do and to present qualitative family research.

There are many sources of the challenges of doing this kind of research, but the most important for the present chapter is intellectual.

Inductive methods are the basis of most qualitative research. LePlay (1855, 1879) one of the first, if not the first, qualitative family researcher, used a form of induction, and its procedures remain fundamental to the analysis of qualitative data. Induction has more than one guise, and in whatever form researchers use it, it helps us analyze the massively detailed data that we gather. What do we do with all that data? How do we organize our data and our findings? How do we demonstrate the bases of our findings? When we learn so much from qualitative inquiry and want others to know what we know, how do we decide what to include in our research reports and what we leave out? The procedures of analytic induction help us respond to these questions.

Such considerations demand sharp analytic skills and immersion in procedures that can help us see what is in the data and that can help us think even more deeply about the data. Bob Bogan (Bogdan & Biklen, 1992), who through his teaching and writing has guided many family researchers in their qualitative analysis, pointed out that qualitative research is about thinking conceptually. He said about his training with Blanche Geer (Becker, Geer, & Hughes, 1968; Becker, Geer, Hughes, & Strauss, 1961) on qualitative methods: "Blanche modeled how to think conceptually. What I got out of her seminar was not the content. She was teaching a way of thinking" (Gilgun, 1992c, p. 9). Glaser (1978) emphasized the centrality of ideas in qualitative research and for sociology in general: "Good ideas contribute the most to the science of sociology" (p. 8). The power of qualitative methods resides in the ideas that guide the research and in the ideas that the methods help develop.

Our personal biographies, however, are intertwined with the intellectual demands of qualitative family research. Often involving close contact with research informants and thus engagement in their hurts and joys, qualitative family research can be emotionally evocative for researchers, stirring up memories and emotions related to our own experiences in our families of origin and our struggles to create our own families. Researchers thus can learn about themselves and be changed by the research (Allen, 1994; Hall & Zvonkovic, 1996). In addition, our personal biographies can play a part in the selection of topics we study and in how we interpret data. LePlay (1879) was clear that his personal history was the impetus for his decades-long research on European working class families. Our social status--gender, race, and class--are becoming increasingly obvious mediators of how we conduct our research and how we interpret findings. The role of personal experience and social location, then, is a theme of this present chapter, and I will trace it from the time of LePlay to today.

In this chapter, I also will deal with how qualitative researchers deal with issues of social change and being social change agents themselves. Do researchers let the data speak for themselves or do

8

researchers become advocates and social reformists on behalf of the persons researched? That is, do we seek to change the difficult human situations that we encounter? These issues have a long history in qualitative family research and are contested today.

These three issues--induction, subjectivity, and social reform--then, are the main methodological foci of this chapter. I will trace these themes from the mid-nineteenth century to the present. I will begin with discussion of how these themes appeared in the work of University of Chicago sociologists, anthropologists, and social workers, move to an examination of the European origins of social research, European origins, and then trace the legacy of the Chicago School of Sociology to the present. The examination of the early years demonstrates the continuities and discontinuities between early, middle, and contemporary family research. Our heritage is a source of generative ideas that will help us shape the future of qualitative family research. Even some of the methodological puzzles of the early years continue to challenge us to our day, despite changes in historical contexts. All three sections illustrate a point Small (1916) made when writing about the first 50 years of sociology, namely, the history of science is not only "the record of discovery of absolutely new facts or truths" but also the reconsideration and recombinations of "ideas long more or less familiar" (p. 723).

In the spirit of the history of qualitative family research, I wrote this chapter in the first person. First-person research accounts were usual during the early years. In his first-person essay, Small (1916) recommended it as means of providing contexts in terms of which future scholars may understand historically-situated research. Many scholars in the Chicago tradition followed his lead.

In this essay, I leave out the important contributions of psychiatry and psychology to the life history (Cohler, 1988; Runyan, 1982), although I emphasize sociology's contributions to life history research, which is an important approach in the Chicago School of Sociology. While this chapter is not an intellectual history of feminist qualitative family research, much of the material I cover is relevant to contemporary feminist thought.

THE HERITAGE
OF QUALITATIVE FAMILY RESEARCH

The history of qualitative family research is difficult to disentangle from the history of qualitative research in general, particularly qualitative sociology. Family researchers until fairly recently were primarily sociologists, and they often were trained in research methods by professors who did not specialize in families. Qualitative family research might not exist at all were if not for the cross-fertilization provided by researchers and methodologists in allied disciplines not necessarily doing research on families. In my version of the heritage of qualitative research, I move back and forth between researchers whose specialty is families and researchers who sometimes did family research and often did other kinds of research, but who influenced qualitative family researchers profoundly or still could potentially.

Since the origins of qualitative family research in mid 1800s until at least until the 1940s, methodological pluralism was the norm. The philosophies of science underlying this pluralism continue to be influential today, although symbolic interactionism and its precursors may be one theoretical orientation that has been most prominent in research on families since the early part of the twentieth century (LaRossa & Reitzes, 1993). Starting perhaps in the late 1940s and 1950s, choices of method appear to have become restricted, a state that only began breaking apart in the last few years.

The Roots of Methodological Pluralism

During the first third or so of the twentieth century, the generative cross-disciplinary thought of many persons closely linked to the University of Chicago came together to produce a flourishing of sociological thought and method (Bulmer, 1984). Founded in 1892, the University of Chicago was well-funded through Rockefeller money and contributions from other wealthy persons. Resources, location in the city of Chicago, and the vision of William Rainey Harper, the first president, attracted some of the most creative and productive academics of the time. Harper's goal was to establish a center of basic research and graduate training (Bulmer, 1984). For Harper, research was primary, and his faculty had far fewer teaching responsibilities than professors at most other institutions. To disseminate research findings, Harper established The University of Chicago Press that developed a series for the academic disciplines, including the Sociological Series, and encouraged the founding of scholarly journals. In the 1890s, Harper recruited John Dewey, George Herbert Mead, and other pragmatist philosophers whose ideas influenced Chicago's social science departments as they were developing during the early part of the twentieth century.

Harper hired Albion Small from his presidency of Colby College in Maine. Small chaired the department of sociology and anthropology for more than 30 years, retiring in 1924 at age 70. At that time, sociology as a discipline was in a formative stage, and Chicago's department was the first. Ruth Cavan (1983), a Ph.D. student in the 1920s, wrote with some hyperbole, "the task fell to this department to define the field of sociology and its methods of study" (p. 409). Within a year, other departments of sociology were founded at Michigan, Kansas, and Columbia. Other universities and colleges soon had their own departments (Faris, 1967). By 1929, sociology became a separate department, but during those decades of association, there was a great deal of cross-over between anthropological research methods and Chicago sociology.

With resources, support from the University administration, and generative ideas current at the University, Small had a major impact on sociology and on research methods. From the beginning, Small "cultivated an eclectic attitude toward current American and European approaches to sociology" (Hammersley, 1989, p. 67). He fostered the view that probing deeply into human actions was more fruitful than the current philosophically-based theorizing (Small, 1916). He encouraged his students to do research in the city of Chicago, whose on-going social transformations formed a naturalistic setting for the urban research that became characteristic of Chicago sociology in later years (Faris, 1967). His thinking meshed with the general pragmatist tenor of the University, and his views were influential not only in his overseeing of the sociology department but in his many other pioneering efforts. Upon Harper's suggestion, he founded the *American Journal of Sociology* in 1895 and was editor until 1924. He was one of the founders of the American Sociological Society, which became the American Sociological Association.

W. I. Thomas, who joined the sociology faculty in 1895, a year before he received his Ph.D. there, expanded the legacies of Small and other Chicago pragmatists. In particular, his work with Florian Znaniecki on *The Polish Peasant in Europe and America*, published between 1918 and 1920, brought to fruition many ideas current at the time. Widely recognized as a landmark in sociological research in general and qualitative family research in particular (Blumer, 1939/1969; Bulmer, 1984; Faris, 1967; Handel, 1992; LaRossa & Wolf, 1985; Rosenblatt & Fischer, 1993), *The Polish Peasant* was based upon personal documents, such as letters, diaries, and life histories; newspaper accounts; and public

11

records. Thomas and Znaniecki (1918-1920/1927) sought to develop "social theory" that "takes into account the whole life of a given society" (p. 18, vol. 1). This holistic perspective includes the personal meanings that individuals give to their social situations, but also encompasses less personal accounts in newspapers and official documents.

Emphasis on Meaning

Emphases on understanding and meanings were been prevalent at Chicago at the time. Many of the Chicago faculty, including Robert Park, a major figure in Chicago sociology, received their Ph.D.'s in German universities and many others studied there, such as Small, Mead, and Thomas. They undoubtedly came into contact with the ideas of Simmel, Kant, and Dilthey, progenitors of many of the ideas underlying Chicago sociology, ideas that are still influential today in interpretive, phenomenological research and the human sciences in general. (See, Dreyfus, 1991; Palmer, 1969; Polkinghorne, 1983; Van Manen, 1990 for a discussion of the human sciences).

Building upon Kant's subjectivist, relativist, and perspectivalist thinking, Dilthey (1976) developed the notion of *Erlebnis*, translated as "lived experience," which he saw as the subject of scientific investigations. For Dilthey, human experience-composed of such intangibles as hopes, emotions, and thoughts--was subject to empirical investigation.

The experiences of individuals compose human social and cultural life, and, conversely, human beings cannot be understood apart from their social and cultural lives. Dilthey agreed with the positivist emphasis on a rigorous empirical basis for research (Palmer, 1969; Polkinghorne, 1983).

The ideas of Kant and Dilthey also centered research efforts on *verstehen*, or understanding, an understanding situated in social, cultural, and historical context, in contrast to Cartesian emphases on explanation, objectivity, and mathematics (Hamilton, 1994). Bulmer (1984) speculated that Thomas and Znaniecki's (1918-1920/1927) emphases on life histories and personal meanings had a "theoretical origin" related to Dilthey, whom he quoted: "Autobiography is the highest and most instructive form in which the understanding of life comes before us" (p. 53, citing Hodges, 1994, p. 29).

Life history accounts not only conveyed personal meanings, but, for Thomas and Znaniecki (1918-1920/1927), they contributed to the science of sociology. They believed that the purpose of science was to reach "generally applicable conclusions." This could be done through studying "each datum" "in its concrete particularity." This, from their view, is the basis of science. They emphasized induction, or the drawing general statements from careful analysis of particular situations:

12

The original subject matter of every science is constituted by particular data existing in a certain place, at a certain time, in certain special conditions, and it is the very task of science to reach, by a proper analysis of these data, generally applicable conclusions. And the degree of reliability of these general conclusions is directly dependent on the carefulness with which each datum has been studied in its concrete particularity (p. 1191).

This is no less true for the study of the individual who must be understood "in connection with his [sic] particular social milieu before we try to find in him [sic] features of a general human interest" (Thomas & Znaniecki, 1927, Vol. 2. p. 1911). Though, as the above excerpt suggests, they valued scientific generalization, they stated that they do not consider their work as giving "any definitive and universally valid sociological truths" (pp, 340-341). Rather, their work is suggestive and prepares the ground for further research.

The following excerpt from a life history demonstrates how a single case can exemplify major social themes. The speaker is a young Polish man in conflict with his parents over their joint business and values relative to the meaning of marriage:

First they [his parents] wanted me to marry any girl whatever provided she had money, and after receiving the dowry they wanted me to give them 300 rubles; then they would go somewhere else and establish a shop and leave me my own bakery. And in leaving they were to take all the contents of the shop. It was well planned, but I was not so stupid as to agree to everything my father wanted. I was rather too good a son, and allowed everything to be done with me, but in the matter of marriage I opposed them positively. I wanted to marry only a girl whom I could really love and in whom I should have a good companion of life. As to giving money to my parents, I thought that we would talk about it when the time came" (Thomas & Znaniecki, 1918-1920/1927, Vol. 2, p. 2174).

Economics versus companionship as a basis for marriage, parental prerogatives, the duties of children, and rebellion against parental expectations are themes in this particular life history, taken at a particular time, in a particular place, from the point of view of a particular individual. Yet, these themes appear throughout decades of family research, a strong argument for their general applicability. These themes also exemplify the young man's lived experience as taking place in a historical, cultural context.

Though Thomas left the University in 1918, his legacy lived on. Almost 60 years later, Cavan (1983) acknowledged not only the contributions of Thomas but those of Ernest Burgess and Robert Park. She wrote of the importance of two books that gave shape to subsequent Chicago sociological research: *The Polish Peasant* and *Introduction to the Science of Sociology,* a textbook written by Park and Burgess (1921), who both joined the faculty in the second decade of the twentieth century. Thomas had a Ph.D. in philosophy from Heidelberg, while Burgess received his Ph.D. in sociology at Chicago (Bulmer, 1984; Faris, 1967).

Research and Lived Experience

Consistent with nineteenth century German philosophy within a human sciences tradition, Park and Burgess (1921) encouraged the development of findings that incorporated the experience of researchers and the points of view of informants, leading their students toward understanding and not toward axiomatic explanatory frameworks. In their textbook, *The Science of Sociology* (1921), they stated that they wanted the text to "appeal to the experience of the student" (p. v), and they advised students to use "their own experience" in recording their observations and in the reading they did for their research (p. vi). Park, in particular, was articulate about the centrality of understanding "the meaning of other people's lives" (quoted by Bulmer, 1984, p. 93). This is done, not solely through intellectual processes, but through imaginative participation in the lives of others. According to Matthews (1977), Park frequently quoted William James: "the most real thing is a thing that is most keenly felt rather than the thing that is most clearly conceived" (p. 33).

Park applied these ideas to his work with students. For example, he advised Pauline Young (1928, 1932) to "think and feel" like the residents of Russian Town, the subject of her dissertation, published in 1932 (Faris, 1967). At the same time, both Burgess and Park emphasized the science and objectivity of the styles of research they were shaping. For us today, emphasizing personal experience and meanings of other persons' lives while considering them part and parcel of an objective science appears to be contradictory. Yet for Park and his colleagues, subjective accounts are proper subjects of scientific research. Researchers become objective insofar as they do not distort findings to serve a reformist agenda. For Park, the disinterested researcher who assembled subjective findings without distortion was displaying objectivity and doing science.

No One Predominant School of Thought

Though symbolic interactionism, which through Blumer (1969/1986) draws upon Pierce, Dewey, Mead, and Cooley, are enduring

14

legacies of the Chicago School of Sociology, Bulmer (1984) pointed out that in the first quarter of the twentieth century, no one school of thought was predominant; rather, the emphasis in Chicago Sociology was the "blending of firsthand inquiry with general ideas" and "the integration of research and theory as part of an organized program" (p. 3). Park had a pungent and direct way of instructing his students to combine first-hand experience with library research and document analysis. Not only did he endorse research that included library research that leads to "a mass of notes," but he also advised his students

to choose problems wherever you can find musty stacks of routine records based on trivial schedules prepared by tired bureaucrats and filled out by reluctant applicants of aid or fussy do-gooders or indifferent clerks.

Noting the dust involved in these enterprises, he told his students that this is "getting your hands dirty in research." He didn't stop here, however:

But one more thing is needful: first hand observation. Go and sit in the lounges of the luxury hotels and on the doorsteps of the flophouses; sit on the Gold Coast settees and on the slum shakedowns; sit in the Orchestra Hall and in the Star and Garter Burlesk. In short, gentlemen [sic], go get the seat of your pants dirty" (McKinney, 1966, p. 71).

Not only does this quote reveal much about Chicago methodology, but it also demonstrates Park's command of the language. Writing well is a legacy of the Chicago School of Sociology. Writing in cogent, evocative terms supports the credibility of qualitative studies. The department held seminars on the use of literature in research, and Park and Burgess encouraged students to read autobiographies and novels (Bulmer, 1984). The research on families done by Chicago sociologists during this time closely followed these approaches, using observation, interviews, and personal document analysis, all of which brings researchers into close contact with social worlds.

Multiple Methods

Park and Burgess encouraged the use of multiple methods and the use of statistics. A typical study used interviewing, observations, document analysis, census data, social mapping and, in the later years, statistical analysis. Social mapping involved locating on maps of Chicago not only distributions of social problems but also locations of residential, undeveloped, and business areas. Students used to joke that they couldn't get their degrees without doing a social map. As Bulmer (1984) documented, Vivien Palmer, who was a senior researcher in the sociology department from 1924 to 1930, also worked closely with the Chicago graduate students, amassed archival material that provided contexts for their urban ethnographies, and wrote the second book on field methods (Palmer, 1928). Examples abound of the plurality of methods used to capture the multiple ecologies of social life in the city. The following are some of them.

The Hobo. Nels Anderson's (1925) *The Hobo*, written for a master's thesis, was the first in the Sociological Series (Faris, 1967). Because of poverty as a graduate student, Anderson lived among hobos--today's counterpart of homeless men--observed them and interacted with them in their daily lives, talked with professionals who worked with them, and elicited life histories. From these sources, both oral and written, he wrote his thesis, arranging his materials in piles on the floor "without misplacing any pages" (Anderson, 1983, p. 404). The result was a classic of sociological research, embodying the principles characteristic of the Chicago School of Sociology.

The Gold Coast and the Slum. At about the same time, Harvey Zorbaugh (1929) was gathering data for *The Gold Coast and the Slum,* a study of juxtaposed, contrasting economic life styles of two Chicago neighborhoods. He used reports from government and social agencies, maps, historical documents, informal contacts with business leaders, with nurses in hospitals, with officials at night court, with newspaper reporters, and door-to-door neighborhood surveys on incomes, rent, and related topics. He organized his findings through social mapping, case studies of members of the social groups he identified, statistical analysis of the financial data, and a social history of the neighborhoods.

Family Disorganization and Domestic Discord. Mowrer's (1927) *Family Disorganization,* based on his 1924 dissertation, and his *Domestic Discord* (Mowrer & Mowrer, 1928), written in collaboration with his wife Harriet Rosenthal Mowrer, used statistics, social mapping, and written documents such as diaries, newspapers, and case study materials taken from records of social workers. In addition, Mowrer and Mowrer linked their findings with previous research and theory and created a theoretical analysis of families under stress.

The Negro Family in Chicago. The methods and methodologies of Frazier's (1932) dissertation *The Negro Family in Chicago* and his later work, *The Negro Family in the United States* (Frazier, 1939) evolved from those in *The Polish Peasant.* Both of these studies used personal documents such as written life histories, and agency case records, interviews, and demographic data. In his Chicago study, Frazier developed a typology: the migrant, the old settler, and the *nouveau riche.* Frazier's purposes in the Chicago study were "insight into the meaning of the world" to the

16

members of these three groups, to gain a "picture of the social and cultural world in which the Negro lives," and "to see the development of the Negro family in relationship to social organization and social control" (p. 258). In brief, he sought to place the "Negro" in a "definite cultural context," so that "he [sic] no longer remains an abstraction in a vacuum as most studies have presented him" [sic] (p. 258). Burgess (1932), in the editor's preface of the Chicago study, noted that Frazier's work exemplified and forecast "a new approach to the more intimate aspects of family and social life" (p. ix). This field study, like others done at about the same time, marked a change from studies of families that were in an institutional and social organizational framework (p. ix).

In *The Negro Family in the United States*, Frazier (1939) used court and archival material, letters, and published autobiographies, in addition to other documents mentioned earlier, to give an account of 150 years of family history within social contexts that included slavery, emancipation, caste-like social status, and migration from rural to urban areas. In the editor's preface, Burgess (1932) called this work "the most valuable contribution to the literature on the family" (p. ix) since the publication more than 20 years earlier of *The Polish Peasant*.

Many other research projects modeled themselves on the methodological diversity characteristic of Chicago research. Charles C. Johnson's (1922) masterful study of *The Negro in Chicago: A Study of Race Relations and a Race Riot in 1919* and Warner and Lunt's (1941) widely recognized *The Social Life of a Modern Community* are a few of many examples of studies within the Chicago tradition but not done by Chicago graduates.

Some Methodological Issues and Dilemmas

Not only were multiple methods, inductive approaches, social processes, urban ecologies, social dislocation, social change, and subjective points of view characteristic of the Chicago School of Sociology, but many researchers were eloquent about methodological dilemmas and issues that are widely discussed today. Mowrer (1932), Dollard (1937), and Anderson (1983) provide examples. Mowrer was interested in the relationships between observations and theory, a theme he addressed repeatedly. This is the regularly debated issue of the difficulties--some say, the impossibility--of induction: how researchers go from concrete observations to concepts and ideas. In *The Family*, yet another volume in the Sociological Series, Mowrer (1932) observed:

But facts are not born full bloom to be plucked by anyone. In every perceptive experience there is an infinite number of observations which might be made but which are not. What the individual sees is determined in part, at least, by what he [sic] is trained to observe....Abstraction thus takes the form of replacing of the actual experiences of the individual by symbols which serve as carriers of what he [sic] considers to be the essential elements of his [sic] experience. Events and objects are grouped by observed regularities or similarities in them. In this third step in scientific method there is always a certain amount of arbitrariness in the selection of what is considered essential, growing out of the training and experience of the researcher (pp. 281-286)

This early formulation of issues related to induction has been a theme in symbolic interactionism and the social sciences in general for generations (Becker, 1988; Blumer, 1939/1969; Hammersley, 1989; Wolcott, 1994). These and other difficulties with induction are bases for those who argue for the superiority of deduction.

John Dollard (Ph.D., University of Chicago, 1930) in his *Caste and Class in a Southern Town,* published in 1937, gave a first-person account that demonstrates that reflexivity in research was an issue then as it is today. For example, Dollard described the social awkwardness of being white in a southern town whose mores forbade treating "Negroes" as equals. Fearing that other white persons were watching as he talked to "Negroes" on his front porch, when he knew their "proper" place was at the back door, he wrote:

My Negro friend brought still another Negro up on the porch to meet me. Should we shake hands? Would he be insulted if I did not, or would he accept the situation? I kept my hands in pockets and did not do it, a device that was often useful in resolving such a situation (p. 7).

This description is a poignant verbal picture of a pivotal moment in Dollard's fieldwork and it is full of connotations about the racist social practices of the time. This excerpt from Dollard illustrates a methodological point Small (1916) made in his essay on the first 50 years of sociological research in the U.S.: namely, the importance of going beyond "technical treatises" and providing first-person "frank judgments" that can help future generations interpret sociology. Without such contexts, "the historical significance of treatises will be misunderstood" (p. 722). Throughout his essay, Small used the first-person and provided his views--or frank judgments--on the events he narrated.

Dollard undoubtedly was building on Small's ideas. In a footnote, Dollard (1937), commented on his use of "I," which he said he used reluctantly, but did so because "it will show the researcher as separate from his data...and it will give the reader a more vivid sense of the research experience" (p. 2). These concerns anticipate contemporary

18

methodological discussions of the role of reflexivity in research.

As shown by the story about not shaking hands with the "Negro," Dollard had an additional reason for using the first person: he wanted to brings issues to life. The use of the "I" became outmoded for decades, and, ironically Chicago graduate William Foote Whyte's (1943) first-person account of "slum sex codes," except for the use of the term *slum*, sounds as if it could have been written today, not only in terms of the information it provides but in terms of its writing style, which is lively and in the first person.

Concern about bias, an issue then and now, also appeared in Dollard's writing. He wrote a chapter on his own biases regarding his study, including a detailed analysis of how an informant, who was a well-known white southern writer, angered him but ultimately helped him become aware of his biases toward white southerners. Subsequent early sociologists have been concerned as well. Waller (1934), for instance, pointed out that prior concepts can help researchers see things they might not have seen but can also blind them to what could be there. Webb and Webb (1932) developed procedures for dealing with researchers' bias, including writing down all of one's ideas, preconceptions, and favorite theories prior to designing the research. They assured researchers if they put aside even their favorite questions and hypotheses, they would find that the processes of direct involvement in the field results in both answers to questions and to testing and verification of hypotheses. Today's qualitative researchers recommend these procedures as well (Bogdan & Biklen, 1992).

In their concern for bias and the place of researchers in research, they were addressing major themes in contemporary epistemological discussions of reflexivity. For instance, Harding (1991), among many others, argues that situating researchers as part of research processes creates a "stronger" and more objective science. Rather than presenting the research through an anonymous narrator whose standpoint is not known, researchers tell much more about their findings when the context the researcher provides is included in research reports.

Concerns About Method

Chicago-trained sociologists made other cogent methodological points. Concerns about methods training and the place of previous research and theory in the conduct of fieldwork plagued Anderson (1925) who presented himself as knowing nothing about method. He kept away from other graduate students because of his felt ignorance. Even after his master's thesis became the first in Chicago's Sociological Series, he characterized himself as a poor researcher, and tongue-in-cheek perhaps, noted that "the book contained not a single sociological concept"(p. 403). His book contains concepts, of course, but not highly abstract concepts and hypotheses; rather, his ideas were embedded in the meanings of the words in his text. Anderson appeared to be making fun of sociologists who may have made a bigger deal over concepts than Anderson thought was necessary for field research.

Dollard (1937) also had concerns about the place of concepts and previous research in his field research. He reported that he did not review pertinent literature until after he finished his study. He deemed it "advisable to try for the advantage which lies in naivete and a freshened perception of the local scene," rather than risk "repeating the well-documented findings of others" (p. 31). In addition, he preferred "to give the reader as deep a sense of participation as may be in what I have heard, seen, and sensed" (pp. 31-32), a theme I discussed earlier and one characteristic of Chicago sociology. Unlike Anderson, then, he found research and theory useful, but only after he completed his research, and, like Waller, he was concerned that his openness to data might be affected by knowledge of the literature. How and when to involve previous research and theory in qualitative studies are of interest in contemporary discussions of qualitative research in general and qualitative family research in particular.

The Seeking of a Statistician

While there was a richness of thought related to field methods and to the methodological challenges that such methods engender, the faculty in sociology did not lose sight of the importance of quantification and statistics. By the mid-1920s, the members of the sociology department saw their lack of expertise in statistics as a weakness and a threat to the national and international stature of their department. They voted unanimously to invite William Ogburn, a leading quantitative sociologist, to join the faculty (Bulmer, 1984). In the late 1920's, there was a flurry of controversy that pitted statistics against case study methods, but within a few years, after many colloquia, journal articles, and long discussions, both professors and students came to view the two approaches as complementary (Faris, 1967). Burgess (1927) and Blumer (1928) made major contributions to this rapprochment. In a 1927 paper on statistics and the case study, for instance, Burgess wrote that statistics and case studies are complementary. Statistics provide correlations and indices, while case studies can reveal social processes and the meanings persons attribute to processes and events that will help "build more adequate statistical indices" (p. 120). The tradition of methodological pluralism most likely created an openness to the new discipline of statistics, and subsequent Chicago-style research usually made ample use of them.

While the Chicago sociologists may have been open to multiple methods, this openness did not maintain itself in sociology in general over the decades. By the 1950s, for instance, even Burgess, identified earlier with field research, was involved almost exclusively in quantitative family research. Other Chicago researchers, however, such as Waller (1934) staunchly maintained that qualitative insight is the basis of knowledge, saw a central place for non-observables such as the imagination and of perception, and continued the tradition of inductive methodologies. Waller wrote, "Quantification is not the touchstone of scientific method. Insight is the touchstone" (p. 288), a view that Cook and Campbell (1979) echoed several decades later when they noted that qualitative knowing underlies all research. Statistics, Waller said, as did Cook and Campbell, serves insight, and experimentation serves the testing and verification of insight.

Waller's (1934) description of the scientific method is similar to later descriptions of analytic induction (Znaniecki, 1934) and of grounded theory (Glaser & Strauss, 1967). Waller wrote that the scientific method was primarily inductive, based on "direct study of human and interhuman behavior....in an attempt to discover recurrent patterns, and, if possible, to make out the entire configuration of events" (p. 289). He assigned a central role to imagination, something few positivists would do, given their emphasis on observables and knowledge based on the senses. Concepts, for Waller, were "transposable perceptual patterns to which we give names" (p. 289). These ideas are current today.

Imagination and the Scientific Method

Waller (1934), like Park, saw a role for imagination in scientific methods and processes, and he compared processes of science to artistic processes:

The application of insight as the touchstone of method enables us to evaluate properly the role of imagination in scientific method. The scientific process is akin to the artistic process; it is a process of selecting out those elements of experience which fit together and recombining them in the mind. Much of this kind of research is simply ceaseless mulling over, and even the physical scientist has considerable need of an armchair (p. 290).

Waller is reminiscent of Kant and Dilthey who recognized the centrality of reflection and the power of thought. Conceptualizations of scientific processes as similar to artistic processes has made many social scientists uncomfortable, but I have found through my own qualitative research that processes of thinking and developing ideas do depend upon

21

imagination and probably are creative processes similar to artistic creativity.

Waller's (1934) thought was consistent with Cooley (1930) when he observed that "our knowledge of human beings is internally as well as externally derived" (p. 294), and he called "imagining what it would be like to be somebody else" a form of "the scientific method" (p. 295). This, of course, is akin to what Blumer (1969/1986) called taking "each other's roles" (p. 9) and is an elaboration of Park's views. Sympathetic understanding as part of the scientific method is very different from the idea of scientific detachment.

The Immediate Context of the Sociology Department

Links between academic settings and the community characterized the early years of Chicago sociology. For example, faculty members such as Dewey, Mead, and Thomas were close associates of Jane Addams, whose Hull House provided a setting and an intellectual atmosphere for the further development of pragmatist thought and methods. The reciprocal influence between academicians and community activists is chronicled in Deegan (1990). According to Deegan, Addams and her associates contributed to Chicago's research methods. Building on the example of Booth's research on the city of London, she and her colleague
s at Hull House did detailed studies of the city of Chicago in the late nineteenth and early twentieth centuries (*Hull-House Maps and Papers*, 1895). These methods of the Hull House group included many subsequently used in Chicago's sociology department.

Addams' ideas of social reform and those of her activist colleagues were compatible with the reformist ideas of the early Chicago pragmatists, who also sought to improve social conditions. Dewey, for example, set up a series of laboratory elementary schools, where he could try out the ideas being developed in the philosophy department (Bulmer, 1984). Addams linked poverty and exploitation of workers with oppressive social and economic conditions, and she was a key figure in such reform movements as standards for occupational safety, the establishment of unions and the support of strikes, and various federal legislation on child labor and family social welfare (Deegan, 1990). Not only was the work of Addams enriched by her association with University of Chicago faculty, but her ideas influenced subsequent developments in sociological research. In addition, Chicago faculty frequently taught courses at Hull House, and residents of Hull House, such as Sophonisba Breckinridge and Edith Abbott (Abbott, 1910; Abbott & Breckinridge, 1916) taught in the sociology department.

Reformist ideas, however, came under heavy criticism for what was seen as their moralistic and paternalistic underpinnings (Bulmer, 1984; Deegan, 1990; Faris, 1967). Sociologists, among them Park and Burgess, disassociated themselves from what they considered "do-gooder" ideologies and the persons whom they viewed as embodying them. Park, showing obvious disrespect for social workers, discouraged his students from taking courses with Abbott and Breckinridge, and he told students in a seminar that "women reformers" have done great damage to the city of Chicago (Bulmer, 1984, p. 68). Abbott and Breckenridge brought the independent School of Civics and Philanthropy to the University in 1920, renaming it the School of Social Service Administration. By the close of the second decade of the twentieth century, there was limited contact between social work eformists and the sociology faculty.

Without the influence of social reformers, Chicago sociology might have taken a different turn (Bulmer, 1984). Under the leadership of Burgess and Park, Chicago sociology was concerned with social problems and the social forces bringing about human oppression and suffering. Their response to social problems was to emphasize the importance of enlightening public opinion, a stance quite different from the social policy, action-oriented research of social workers. Ironically, Park was a social reformer of highest repute. He worked for almost a decade as Booker T. Washington's secretary. He nurtured some major research on African-American social problems, such as Charles C. Johnson's (1922) *The Negro in Chicago: A study of race relations and a race riot in 1919* and Frazier's work discussed earlier. He chaired Chicago's Urban League and spent the last seven years of his life at Fiske University in Atlanta, a traditional black institution (Bulmer, 1984). Like Le Play who will be discussed later, Park kept his reformist ideas separate from his research and research advising.

The European Origins of Research on Families

Addams and her associates contributed to Chicago sociology, and other early social reformists did as well. These reformists include Charles Booth, Beatrice and Sidney Webb, and E. S. Rowntree in England and Frederic LePlay, a French metallurgist and social scientist who did research on families and their economic status throughout Europe in the second quarter of the nineteenth century. They developed a multi-methods approach that later characterized Chicago sociology, such as social surveys, in-depth interviews, participant observation, document analysis, analysis of demographic data, and social mapping. Booth (1903), for example, pinpointed taverns and churches on a detailed map of the city of London, in order to facilitate understanding of the relationships between "drunkenness," religion, and family poverty. Wax

(1971), a Chicago trained anthropologist, reported that Burgess and Park used Webb and Webb's (1932) *Methods of Social Study* in their field methods seminar. In this book, the authors, who worked closely with Booth and shared his reformist ideals, describe participant observation, methods of dealing with researcher bias, and inductive methods of data analysis and interpretation.

A typical method was participant observation, which did not have that name yet. A tactic of the research was to tap into a wide variety of points of view. Booth (1903) described a participant observation: his researchers took "long walks in all parts of London day after day with picked police officers who were permitted to assist us during the revision of our maps" (p. 61). He sought "diversities of opinion affected by the point of view of the observer, as well as by the class observed." He, therefore, presented his findings as "a patchwork of quotations...drawn from the clergy, ministers of religion, and missionaries, from schoolmasters and others" (p. 60). Park frequently took his students on long walking tours of Chicago neighborhoods, and, as discussed earlier, emulated methods based on diverse sources of data.

Booth (1903), however, freely labeled social conditions "evil," tried to identify sources of responsibility, and sought to change conditions, qualities that may have offended later researchers who valued a more detached stance. The following illustrates his perspectives: "In considering this subject [housing] I shall first enumerate the evils and try to allocate responsibility, and then indicate the efforts that are being made to improve matters, and their results" (p. 158). Then and now, researchers with a social reform--or critical, emancipatory--stance may find his language quaint, but essentially agree with him. Here again is a contrast between reform-minded researchers on the one hand and basic researchers on the other. Park and Burgess (1921), however, praised Booth's work as an example of "disinterested investigation" (p. 44) that threw "great light, not only upon poverty in London, but upon human nature in general" (p. 45). Approvingly, they noted that this mammoth study "raised more questions than it settled," and they agreed with Booth when he said that the problems need to be better stated (Booth, 1889). They apparently did not see his reformist ideas affecting his objectivity.

First Use of Field Methods in Sociology

Frederic LePlay, the earliest of the social reformists and the first to employ field methods in sociology, did the most extensive research on families and social conditions that has ever been done. His field research began in 1829 and ended in the 1850s, with the 1855 publication of *Les ouvriers europeens*. His contributions to sociology are monumental and well documented by Silver (1982) who also noted that in later years, LePlay's contributions eventually were discounted, not only because of the dominance of statistical methods but because of the general distaste for his reformist ideas and possibily a mistrust of inductive methods. By the 1930s, academics such as philosopher Mortimer Adler, were advocating deductive methodologies and condemning induction as "bad science" (Bulmer, 1984, p. 203).

LePlay was driven by his concern for human suffering, but he did not present his reformist ideas in *Les ouvriers europeens*. Like Park several decades later, he assumed that his ideas and findings would speak for themselves and lead to social reform. When he saw that this didn't happen, he devoted the last decades of his life to social activism, seeking ways to apply his ideas to social interventions. In the course of doing so, he wrote several other books and produced a new edition of *Les ouvriers* (LePlay, 1879). His fieldwork, however, ended by the 1850s, and he died about 30 years later in 1882.

Trained as an engineer and metallurgist, LePlay applied the scientific methods of his day to the study of families during times of great social and economic changes. The methods of his research, like the research that succeeded his, continue to be viable today. These include inductive reasoning based on direct and prolonged contact with the empirical world and the centrality of his personal history to his choice of topic and method. Institutional support for his research enabled him to do his decades-long fieldwork.

Induction as Scientific Method

LePlay deliberately based his social research methods on his training as an engineer and metallurgist, or "the scientific method." In LePlay's terms, this was an method of observation and reasoning that leads to the "truth" (in French, *au vrai*). He noted that "the method is as old as the human species and practiced by eminent men [sic] long before Descartes, Bacon, and Aristotle, recommended it to philosophers" (LePlay, 1866, p. 3). He held up the practice of the chemist as a model for doing research, and it was this type of research in which he had confidence.

This, of course, is the method of induction. His inductive, observational methods contrasted with the speculative, deductive methods prevalent in his time (Silver, 1982). In his own words, LePlay was repelled by the "blind propaganda of the salons" (LePlay, 1879, Vol. 1, p. 47) and the unverified moral precepts of the social reformists (Silver, 1982). He wrote, "In scientific matters, only direct observation of facts can lead to rigorous conclusions and to their acceptance" (LePlay, 1879, Vol. 6, translated by Silver, 1982, p. 179). For

25

LePlay, observations are verified many times. For instance, after almost 20 years of research, he went back into the field for seven more years to check and revise his findings in preparation for the publication of *Les ouvriers* (Silver, 1982). Through observation, classification, and induction, he sought "the principles of social science" (Zimmermann & Frampton, 1935 p. 567).

His approach in social research was to do in-depth studies of families in many countries before he came to any conclusions. He completed about 300 studies of families, which he called monographs, with the assistance of 100 other researchers. The methods were observation--including living with families from a week to a month at a time, interviewing family members, and then interviewing a variety of public officials who knew the family members.

His initial efforts were marked by confusion. Unfamiliarity with languages and the "complexity and variety of facts" with which he was confronted unsettled him (Silver, 1982, p. 160), but he eventually managed and made sense of his observations. He lived with families "to understand their language and their life" (Zimmerman & Frampton, 1935, p. 473). He learned to speak several languages in the course of his studies. To organize data collection, he developed a framework consisting of 16 topics, such as description of the setting in which the family lived, family demographics, family history, family social status, food and meals, health and hygiene, and family economics.

The framework is a prior conceptualization, against which he railed. Pragmatically, however, he needed it to organize his unruly findings. His discussions of interviewing suggests a middle road between imposing ideas on social life and an entirely inductive method:

Questioning should be conducted in the order indicated by the method. Nevertheless, this order must not be followed too rigorously. The workingman [sic] will naturally tend to elaborate on certain subjects: he [sic] will enjoy related memories of his [sic] youth and telling his [sic] family history. It is important not to interrupt him [sic], so that useful information will not be lost....It is much better to listen than to ask questions (LePlay, 1862, translated by Silver, 1982, p. 182)

In his procedures, then, he allowed new material to emerge. Yet, the framework was probably indispensable in guiding the research. It also provided the organizational structure for the presentation of the findings. LePlay was in tune with a principle that methodologists since at least the time of Durkheim (1966) have recognized: namely, the importance of general principles to guide data collection and interpretation.

Trust in Research Processes

Giving much thought to the influence of pre-conceived ideas on his own research, LePlay expressed confidence that research processes would take care of this problem. He stated that it is common for observers to begin their studies seeking to find facts that fit their "erroneous" principles, but the method itself will lead to correct conclusions (Silver, 1982, p. 181). In addition, working with other researchers "removed" "error arising from preconceived ideas" (Zimmerman & Frampton, 1935, p. 377). How exactly these processes work was not spelled out.

This reticence about research procedures is characteristic of the work of our predecessors. Leonard Schatzman (Schatzman & Strauss, 1973; Shatzman, 1991) who taught grounded theory, a form of qualitative research for more than 30 years, said in an interview:

In the history of qualitative research, most professors couldn't articulate the method. A student would ask a prof, 'Where did you get that concept?' The prof would mumble something and then add, 'Hang around a few years, and you'll see.' Sure enough, the student would hang around for a couple of years and would see. The student becomes a professor and her student asks, 'Where did you get that concept?' The prof mumbles something and then says, 'Hang around a few years. You'll see' (Gilgun, 1993a, p. 1).

This reticence began to change in 1967 with the publication of Glaser and Strauss's *The Discovery of Grounded Theory*, and today researchers are much more articulate about research procedures. Nonetheless, the essential ambiguity of induction may be intractable.

Faith in--or the trustworthiness of--the processes of induction may be increased by repeated observations, multiple interpreters, and the interplay between hypothesis generation and testing. For example, 15 years into his research, LePlay came to believe that he had developed some "principles of social science drawn by inductions from the facts observed." He concluded that "there was no longer any occasion to add anything to them by observing new facts" (Zimmerman & Frampton, 1935, p. 573). Glaser and Strauss (1967) would call this theoretical saturation. Few researchers take 15 years to reach saturation. The scope of LePlay's project was so broad that it took a decade and a half. Few researchers undertake such far-ranging projects and reach a point where they have credible findings much sooner than that.

Despite not learning anything new about European families, LePlay noted that he was not able to formulate the social science principles he sought with the "clearness which I am now able to give them" (Zimmerman & Frampton, 1935, p. 573). This statement, from a man who was in the field for more than 20 years and was brilliant enough to finish four years of study at the *Ecole des mines* in two years, clearly articulates the difficulties of formulating principles derived from inductive research. Interpretation of qualitative data requires much thought, as discussed earlier, and time in which to reflect.

Personal History

LePlay wrote an autobiography published as the first chapter in volume one of the second edition of *Les ouvriers* (LePlay, 1879). He did so to demonstrate that his method was not based on pre-conceived ideas, arguing instead that his ideas arose from his life experiences. In this sense, he saw living his life as personal fieldwork, an inductive process, through which he developed his own guiding ideas, primary among which was the relief of human suffering. In the autobiography, LePlay discussed the effect on him of economic depressions, social upheavals, and revolutions that characterized France in the eighteenth and nineteenth centuries. During LePlay's childhood, his uncle and friends of his uncle instructed him on the social and political history of France, and they strongly were on the side of the common people. In 1830, disabled by a laboratory accident, he listened to his friends discuss the Napoleonic revolutions and heard and saw the turmoil from his window. He wrote, "When I saw the blood spilled by the July Revolution [of 1830], I dedicated my life to the restoration of social harmony in my country" (LePlay, 1879, Vol. 1, p. vii). The more remote influences were the childhood years that he spent in the countryside among French working families, times he recalled with great warmth. He affectionately recalled his mother, who read books with him during his childhood. LePlay, then, is part of a long tradition of using autobiographical material to generate ideas for research.

Silver (1962) saw contradictions between LePlay's views that his research did not reflect preconceived ideas and his stance that his personal experiences influenced him profoundly. How much of an issue this actually is may be hard to pin down. Today, it is generally assumed that personal experiences influence research processes (Sollie & Leslie, 1994). Researchers have standpoints, as do readers (Allen, 1994). The meanings of texts do not depend solely upon the intentions and methods of the writers of texts (Barthes, 1974). Readers, however, often appreciate knowing writers' personal experiences to aid in interpretive processes. For today's post-structuralists, the interpretations of readers take precedence over the intentions of writers (Barthes, 1974; Gilgun, 1995a; Noth, 1995). While LePlay appeared to believe that the truth is out in the world waiting to be discovered, more contemporary qualitative researchers take a social constructivist, post-structuralist view that ourselves as well as "what is out there" are forms of texts to which we give meaning (Barthes, 1974; Manning & Cullum-Swan, 1994).

Institutional Support

LePlay enjoyed institutional support for his research. For 25 years, the French Ministry of Public Works gave him six months of paid leave from his professorship at the Ecole des Mines to do his social science research. Harper's release of the University of Chicago faculty from teaching to allow them to do research is another example of institutional support that had great dividends. Today, released time for research remains a boon for academic researchers.

Summary

In its origins, the methods of research on families were primarily but not exclusively inductive. The methods engaged researchers in the worlds of informants through personal documents, participant observation, and interviewing, and they were respectful of quantification which often provided some of the context in which to interpret findings. They often used official documents and demographic data to flesh out their understandings. That persons interact with their social environments in terms of mutually influencing processes was assumed. Earlier researchers sought the points of view of informants, although some, such as LePlay, did not include other "voices" in his research but instead was an omniscient and detached narrator, much in the manner of most of today's positivistic research reports. Thomas, at the end of the nineteenth century and into the twentieth, was one of the earliest to demonstrate the significance of personal meanings of informants, a perspective based on nineteenth century German philosophy.

Scores of subsequent Chicago sociological researchers took up these views, and they eventually became part of symbolic interactionism and other interpretive methodologists, including those who consider themselves part of a human sciences tradition. The early sociologists discussed enduring methodological dilemmas and sometimes consciously attempted to invite readers into the experience of these dilemmas, such as the meanings of doing research in an unfamiliar culture, the place of concepts in research, confronting and managing bias, and the place of social reform sentiments, the latter appearing today in emancipatory, critical stances. Chicago sociologists are part of a human sciences tradition, although further scholarship is necessary to see whether these researchers so situated themselves.

The Chicago sociologists did not consider their theories to be universal and applicable independent of time, place, and person. Rather,

29

they were aware of situational boundedness of ideas, and, indeed, were probably influenced by historicist theories that made that very point. As Thomas and Znaniecki (1918-1920/1927) pointed out in their methodological note, their findings are not universal but simply prepare the ground for further inquiry. They were interested in understanding persons in historical situations and their theories were meant to illuminate social processes.

Many contemporary qualitative researchers are doing their work without knowing the richness of their own heritage. The roots of qualitative family research go deep, to the origins of empirical research. This review of the early history of qualitative family research hopefully will help establish for qualitative family researchers that not only do we have a rich tradition on which to build but as qualitative researchers we have a central place in family studies.

THE TRADITION ENDURES:
THE "MIDDLE YEARS"

Though other methods and methodologies eventually became ascendent, sociologists and members of other disciplines trained at Chicago from the 1920s to the 1960s carried on the tradition. For instance, the writings of Glaser and Strauss (Glaser, 1978; Glaser & Strauss, 1967; Strauss, 1997; Strauss & Corbin, 1990) are replete with statements about the importance of methodological pluralism and the self-evident nature of researchers' subjective engagements with informants and the meanings of their data. Glaser (1978), for instance, stated about methodological pluralism:

"*Our perspective is but a piece of a myriad of action in Sociology, not the only right action*.... The division of labor in sociology needs *all* perspectives on styles of both theoretical and empirical renderings of research data (p. 3, emphasis in original text).

Glaser (1978) stressed the centrality of the "social psychology of the analyst" and noted that "Generating theory is done by a human being who is at times intimately involved with and other times quite distant from the data--and who is surely plagued by other conditions in his [sic] life" (p. 2). This is a clear statement on the role of reflexivity in research. Glaser and Strauss, whose primary work was medical sociology, assume that the results of their research will be applied and used to ameliorate personal and social ills.

Other researchers, too, made such assumptions. Much of the

work of researchers in the Chicago tradition focused on research for social amelioration and social change, a thrust similar to their European and American predecessors. Examples of research related to families and social change are Cavan and Ranck's (1938) *The Family and the Depression*, Rainwater, Coleman, and Handel's (1959) *Workingman's Wife*, Hess and Handel's (1959) *Family Worlds*, Komarovsky's (1940, 1962) *The Unemployed Man and his Family* (1940) and *Blue Collar Marriage* (1962), and Lopata's series of studies on women's occupations (1971, 1973, 1979, 1984, 1985, 1992a, 1996).

During these middle years from the late 1930s to the mid-1980s, Chicago continued to have an interdisciplinary faculty and graduate students who were drawn to Chicago's traditional styles of research. The writing of Rosalie Wax (1971), a Chicago graduate with a Ph.D. in anthropology, demonstrates how methodological ideas espoused by Park, Thomas, and others of the Chicago school earlier in the twentieth century, continued to be developed. The work of English anthropologist Elizabeth Bott (1957/71) on couples' social network shared methodologies with the Chicago tradition, and she later became a faculty member at Chicago. Bott, with Znaniecki (1934), Lindesmith (1947), Cressey (1953), and Glaser and Strauss (1967), played major roles in the on-going articulation of inductive procedures characteristic of qualitative research.

Chicago graduates and former Chicago faculty fanned out across the United States to create small pockets of graduate students and professors who sustained the tradition. For instance, Anselm Strauss went to the University of California-San Francisco in 1968 to form the department of social and behavioral sciences. There he recruited like-minded faculty, such as Barney Glaser, Leonard Schatzman, Fred Davis, and Virginia Olesen. This faculty trained generations of nursing and sociology students, with Strauss, Glaser, and Schatzman having decades-long responsiblity for training in research methods and methodologies. As will be shown in the third section of this essay, nursing researchers today are among the most productive qualitative family scholars. Chicago graduates Howard Becker spent most of his career at Northwestern, Blanche Geer had several academic jobs including at Syracuse University where she was Bob Bogdan's (Bogdan & Biklen, 1992) advisor, and Erving Goffman was at Berkeley. Jacqueline Wiseman (1979, 1981, 1991), a qualitative family researcher, is one of Goffman's students. Blumer also was at Berkeley for many years.

Nursing and sociology students at the University of California-San Francisco routinely took courses at Berkeley with Blumer, Goffman, and such phenomenologically-oriented philosophers as Hubert Dreyfus (1991), Jane Rubin (1988), and Martin Packer (Packer, 1985; Packer & Addison, 1989), all of whom have had a major influence. In some ways, the Berkeley area during these middle years and into contemporary times replicated the intellectual atmosphere of the University of Chicago in the early part of this century.

Helena Lopata's Graduate School Years

A sense of the continuities and transformations of Chicago traditions are part of the life history accounts of Helena Lopata (1992b), who was a student at Chicago from 1945 to 1954, and Gerald Handel (Gilgun, 1992a), who received his Ph.D. in human development in 1962. Lopata emphasized theoretical issues such as role theory and sensitizing concepts and appeared less focused on method, as if her method is self-evident, which it undoubtedly was to her and the tradition in which she learned and practiced research. From her Chicago sociology professors, she received the same directives that Park gave his students decades earlier. An immigrant from Poland, she wanted to study Polish immigrant family life in the U.S. She said her professors

told [me] to go to Polonia--and actually talk with the people, attend meetings, and even collect questionnaires? I went (Lopata, 1992b, p. 1).

She was open about her "reformist" attitude--that is, her interest in social change, aroused while she at the University of Chicago. An immigrant from Poland, she stated in her life history her concern about the response to Nazism in the midwestern United States:

Speeches given around the midwest about Naziism and the crucial need for clothing and money for medicine to send back to Europe met with total indifference and ignorance. I ended up doing a master's thesis on "International Cooperation in Medicine," probably to convince myself that cooperation is possible in the world (Lopata, 1992b, p. 1).

She showed no trace of self-consciousness about the personal meanings of this and subsequent research projects. Lopata had no courses on research methods, but learned methods of procedure through course lectures, reading theory and research reports, and through her field experience.

Gerald Handel and Creative, Independent Thinking

When Handel was a student at Chicago, he, too, had no formal training in research methods, but he was enchanted by the Chicago emphasis on interpretation. Like Lopata, he found that students were expected to be independent scholars in close contact with informants and the worlds in which they lived. Handel's work is embedded in interactionism and his interest is in the meanings that informants attribute to their situations.

My account of Gerald Handel's experiences as a student at the University of Chicago is based on an interview (Gilgun, 1992a). Besides the works cited earlier, Handel is co-editor with Kerry Daly and me of *Qualitative Methods in Family Research*. His other publications include the study of whole families (Handel, 1996; 1965; Hess & Handel, 1959), the psychosocial interior of the family (Handel, 1967; Handel & Whitchurch, 1993), childhood socialization (Handel, 1988), and case studies (Handel, 1991).

Handel studied with Carl Rogers, Bruno Bettleheim, Lloyd Warner, and Elizabeth Bott in an exemplary interdisciplinary program. He said he regrets not taking Everett Hughes' research course in which each student was assigned a census tract and had to find out everything possible about that tract: qualitative and quantitative data, the subcultures, the institutions, demographics. This, of course, is part of the Chicago methodological tradition of social mapping. For Handel, the environment at Chicago was demanding and creative, and students were surrounded with faculty who were at the height of their careers, creating new insights through interpretive activities. He was immersed in exciting new ideas that inspired him in his own research. As he said:

Each of us had to come to our own interpretation of the material. No one would do it for us. Bettelheim was developing his own ideas, Carl Rogers was doing his thing, and Warner was developing his ideas about American communities. Individuals as rooted in society was a core idea at Chicago....The act of interpretation was a central activity. Interpreting symbols--that's what Freud did. That's what G. H. Mead said was important. Warner's course based on his studies of Yankee City was subtitled *The Symbolic Life of America*. He had an analysis of the symbolic organization of a Memorial Day parade in Yankee City--what kind of floats people produced and who was allowed to do what. He interpreted the symbolic meaning of the floats. This was an extraordinary analysis.

Another was on the social organization of the cemetery--who's buried where and how. It was amazing stuff to us. These ideas were very, very innovative. One way or another, among the work we studied, the intellectual activity was interpreting human behavior: Freud, Erikson, G. H. Mead, Piaget, and Warner (Gilgun, 1992a, p. 5).

Handel struggled with the notion that the ideas being presented in class and through reading often did not match up with what was called research. "Here I was reading [and studying with] those magnificent, insightful thinkers," Handel said, "and then there was this other kind of [quantitative] literature which was smaller in scale." Handel said,

33

"Students who did quantitative work puzzled me. My question was, Why were they doing that?" Excited by ideas and inductive processes of working with ideas, Handel could not connect with the thinking behind quantitative studies. Handel did not take courses on qualitative interviewing, which was his main method of data collection. "I was not explicitly trained, " he said. "It's a mystery how I absorbed it. Somehow I absorbed it, probably through the notion of whose ideas were important to me--G.H. Mead, Freud, M. Mead, Erikson, Piaget."

Students together in human development, Hess and Handel co-wrote a proposal to the National Institute of Mental Health, which was funded. That research was written up as *Family Worlds*, based on in-depth qualitative interviews with each member of 33 families. They also used the projective Thematic Apperception Test. This work blended Burgess's (1926) notion of family interaction with Chicago's emphasis on multiple methods and personal meanings in interpretations of situations. Through primarily inductive analysis, they formulated five processes of family interaction and functioning: patterns of separation and connectedness; notions of individual and family images; family themes; family boundaries; and the meanings of age and gender to each family member. These ideas have been applied in a wide range of theoretical and applied settings (Handel, 1996; LaRossa & Reitzes, 1993; Rosenblatt & Fischer, 1993).

Other Excellent Qualitative Research

Many other well-known qualitative studies were published during these middle years. Some were based on large-scale surveys, were concerned with representativeness and generalizability, and had much in common with quantified surveys (e.g., Rainwater et al, 1959), demonstrating once more the methodological pluralism that had characterized family research almost from the beginning. Others classic family research at that time include Komarovsky's (1962) studies of families and class where she documented the centrality of mother-daughter ties and Lillian Rubin's (1976) profoundly emotive accounts of the pain of living at the edge of poverty. Rubin's background as a psychotherapist, her clinical interviewing skills, and her experience growing up in a poor family contributed to the depth of her study, which was unique for the time, but was consistent with the methodological perspectives of the early Chicago School of Sociology. Anthropologists of the family also had great impact. Among them are Lewis (1962, 1963, 1964, 1965) on Mexican families and Stack (1974) on African-American kinship systems. These studies and other continued to remind the research community of the value of qualitative research methods.

The theory developed during these middle years continues to be influential to our day. Boss's (1987) account of the history of the concept *family stress* is an example of how major family theories rest on the bedrock of inductive research conducted during these middle years. According to Boss, contemporary notions of family stress were based on the work of Cavan and Ranck (1938) and Angell (1936) on families and the Depression. Both used inductive case study methods. Angell identified and defined the concepts of family integration and adaptability as important to how families respond to the stress of a sudden loss of income. His analysis, according to Boss, "remains unchallenged today" (p. 696), and, as important, are recognized as relevant in current deductive research.

Cavan and Ranck (1938) supported Angell's conclusions. They found that well-organized families under economic stress "continued to be organized, whereas disorganized families became further disorganized (Boss, 1987, p. 696). Other researchers over time successfully built on this seminal work. Boss lists the qualitative research of Komarovksy (1940), Koos (1946), Angell (1936), and Cavan and Ranck (1936) as the foundation of Hill's (1949) model of family stress, which he elaborated using case study and survey methods. In addition, Hill incorporated the notion of meaning into his theory of family stress; that is, the meanings and significance that events have to family members are central to whether or not an event is experienced as stressful.

For many of today's family researchers, Reuben Hill is an icon, and his early work rests solidly on Chicago-based researchers with its methodological pluralism and the centrality of meaning. Boss's own research (Boss, 1988; Flavel & Boss, 1992) and that of McCubbin (McCubbin, Cauble, & Patterson, 1984; McCubbin & Thompson, 1989; McCubbin, Thompson, Thompson, & Fromer, 1994) both well-known for research and theory on family stress, have built on the research of the middle years, including Hill's work. As Boss (1987) pointed out, however, research on meaning requires qualitative methods, and the reluctance of researchers to use these methods may be a reason why we know so little about the meanings family members attribute to events that could be stressful. Undoubtedly, there are many generative family theories originating from inductive, case study methods. Boss's (1987) analysis provides one example.

Continual Mutual Influences

Mutual influences between anthropology and sociology continued in these middle years. The work of Rosalie Wax, a Chicago Ph.D. in anthropology, and English social anthropologist Elizabeth Bott (1957/1971) illustrate this point. Wax continued Chicago's tradition of reflecting on methodological issues related to subjectivity, particularly in her classic fieldwork text (Wax, 1971) that embodies many of the ideas circulating at the University of Chicago. In her preface, she thanked, among others, the Chicago sociologist Everett Hughes. In her presentation of fieldwork, she incorporated her biography, which is a traditional Chicago approach, as shown earlier. Her stated purpose was pedagogical: to train "future generations of fieldworkers" (p. x). This view is solidly in the Chicago tradition of speaking in the first-person in order to provide historical contexts that aid in interpretation, articulated by Small (1916) early in the twentieth century and sustained over the ensuing decades. She shared her "pre-college life experiences," such as how she earned a living during the Depression, how she managed her life as a junior college student, and how she learned about cultural variations as a child. These and other autobiographical details situated Wax within her text and helped in its interpretation.

Wax was concerned with "*shared* meanings" (p. 11), which she saw as preconditions for understanding, her view of the purpose of fieldwork. This, of course, is within the human sciences tradition and fits well with Chicago traditions. For Wax, researchers attain understanding through personal experience; that is, a re-socialization into the culture under consideration, a stance Park imparted to his students and probably based on his training in German philosophy. Wax gave many examples of re-socialization but noted that researchers remain outsiders.

Wax recognized that resocialization may entail personal transformations, an insight Wax (1971) attributed to Malinowski. In other words, participation in research processes can change researchers. In some cases, researchers become social reformists, a theme in the early qualitative family research of such persons as LePlay and Booth. She noted that as a result of their field work, she and her anthropologist husband Murray "became moral protagonists of Indian communities" (p. 41), that Alfred Lindesmith became an opponent of harsh narcotic laws after his research on opium addicts, and that many other social researchers found that fieldwork "undermined" the "pretence of moral neutrality" (p. 41). She acknowledged that these transformations met with approval by some but "antagonized" those who "defined science as pure" (p. 41). Wax built upon some major themes within the Chicago tradition and transformed others, such as her frank statement of advocacy as an outcome of research. Some contemporary phenomenological nursing researchers view her work as influential on their own, as SmithBattle attested (L. SmithBattle, personal communication, 1996). In contemporary work, there also is an awareness of the effect of research on researchers, not only in terms of methodological and often feminist discussions of reflexivity (Sollie & Leslie, 1994), but also in data-based research reports (cf; Gilgun, 1995a & b; Hall & Zvonkovic, 1996; Stacey, 1990).

Elizabeth Bott and Inductive Research Processes

The work of English anthropologist Elizabeth Bott (1957/1971) on couples' social networks was quite different from that of Wax. While Wax emphasized shared meanings and researchers' resocialization, Bott's focus was on theory development. In her work, she illustrated the interplay between induction and deduction in the conduct of qualitative family research. Her work anticipates many of today's research methods, particularly grounded theory (Glaser & Strauss, 1967), a form of induction. Terming her research *exploratory*, Bott did not begin her study with "well-formed hypotheses" but had the general goal of "psychological understanding of some ordinary urban families" (Bott, 1957/9711, p. 8). She said she and her team "succumbed to the confusion" of open-ended research "in the hope that constant careful comparisons would eventually lead to a formulation of specific problems" (p. 9). Bott not only anticipated the methods of grounded theory, but she even used the term *constant comparison*, a term Glaser and Strauss later used.

Having no hypotheses does not mean that the research was atheoretical and unguided by concepts. Bott's theoretical framework was Lewin's field theory (1935, 1936), which holds that behavior is a function of person and environment. This, of course, is a variation of ecological theory and consistent with the interactionist perspectives that characterized the Chicago School of Sociology from its inception. Lewin's concepts undoubtedly were sensitizing (Blumer, 1954/1969), helping Bott and her team to identify and name processes they might never have noticed otherwise. For Blumer, sensitizing concepts give researchers "a general sense of reference and guidance in approaching empirical instances" (p. 148). In other words, sensitizing concepts orient researchers to the analysis and interpretation of data, as Lopata showed in her intellectual life history and is routine for most researchers within Chicago traditions.

Doing her research during a time when probability theory and deductive research were in ascendence, Bott (1957/1971) made important methodological points about the generalizability of her findings and the nature of the hypotheses that result from studies such as hers. Her sample of 20 urban families, Bott noted, was neither representative nor random. Whether any facts that such research uncovers were typical was not her concern. What was of concern were hypotheses, which she saw as possibly "generalizable to other families but require further testing" (p. 10), not only on English families but on families in other societies. In short, she saw the kind of research she did as a way of developing viable, testable theory. She pointed out that such hypotheses are written in

37

general terms so as to permit testing. Thomas and Znaniecki (1918-1920/1927), Lindesmith (1947), Znaniecki (1934), among others, articulated similar views on the generalizability of inductive research.

As unorthodox for the times as her research was, Bott's results were well received and set off a series of studies and papers that Bott (1959/1971) chronicled in a long chapter at the end of the second edition of *Family and Social Network*. Her work continues to be quoted in contemporary research on social networks. Bott was aware of how different her research was and conceded that some may find it difficult to accept. When Bott presented her preliminary analyses to Max Gluckman's seminar on social anthropology at the University of Manchester, England, and asked the seminar participants what to do with her material, Gluckman and one participant said simultaneously "Write a novel about it" (Gluckman, 1971, p. xiv). Gluckman later admitted he was wrong and called her work "one of the most illuminating analyses ever to emerge from social anthropology" (p. xiv).

Blending Induction and Deduction

The place of pre-conceived ideas in inductive procedures has intrigued qualitative researchers over the decades. Bott (1957/1971) was not clear about when sensitizing concepts entered her research. Others are very clear, such as Schatzman's account of the discovery of the theory of "negotiated order" and Lindesmith's (1947) use of hypotheses in his study of opium addiction. In an interview (Gilgun, 1993a), Schatzman demonstrated the use of sensitizing concepts and showed that they do not preclude discoveries of new theories:
'The theory of negotiated order (Strauss, Schatzman, Bucher, Ehrlich, & Sabshin, 1962) grew out of our Chicago psychiatric study,' he said. 'We applied sensitizing concepts, the usual stuff of the social organization of a hospital, having to do with rule and norms. Strauss, in discussion with Schatzman, Rue Bucher, and other members of the research team, was saying, "Yeah, yeah, there are rules and norms in this hospital. What else is going on here?" We came up with the negotiation concept. There are rules, but rules are negotiated, rules are bent, broken, ignored, argued over, all within the negotiation process. We literally declared that modern organizations are better regarded as negotiated processes where rules are constantly being negotiated and re-negotiated. It isn't that the rules are not there or not fair--it is rather that rules and norms are in flux.
'We looked at each other, and we gasped and said, "Gee, that's a theory." Put in your thumb and pull out a plum and say what a good boy am I. We dared publish it that way, and it rang a bell. Terrific. I know

there are rules. We set that aside and said rules are not central. What is central is how these people deal with each other and negotiate problems day to day' (p. 5).

In this description of inductive processes that lead to a new concept and theory, Schatzman is clear that the research team used "prior conceptualizations" which were concepts taken from symbolic interactism and role theory. Schatzman called these concepts *sensitizing*, using the term as Blumer (1954/1969) recommended. Though Strauss's research team used sensitizing concepts, they did not have a clue at the onset of their research that they would discover the concept of negotiated order. Schatzman conveyed the astonishment and joy the team experienced in their discovery. As Schaztman's account shows, the use of sensitizing concepts and hypotheses does not preclude the discovery of new ideas (Gilgun, 1995b), or what Glaser and Strauss (1967) have termed *emergence* of theory grounded in data that are gathered inductively.

Grounded Theory Analysis

As conceptualized by Strauss, Glaser, and Corbin (Glaser & Strauss, 1967; Glaser, 1970, 1992; Strauss, 1987; Strauss & Corbin, 1990), the procedures of grounded theory analysis involve sensitizing concepts that guide researchers in a conscious effort to discover what can be considered latent, or core, variables which underlie descriptions of social phenomena. The notion of "negotiated order" is an example of a core variable. These core variables are identified, the possibility of multi-dimensionality are explored, the consequences of these processes are investigated, and, finally, the conditions, or the social contexts, under which these processes occur are identified (Strauss & Corbin, 1990). Grounded theory as developed over the years by Strauss and his associates, then, is a set of procedures designed to build substantive, or middle-range theories. To build a more generally applicable theory, Glaser and Strauss (1967) suggest constructing theory inductively across substantive areas.

Glaser and Strauss have been interpreted as eschewing any use of pre-conceived ideas. Yet, in their 1967 text, they instruct researchers in Lazarfeld's elaboration theory which involves investigating "conditions, consequences, dimensions, types, processes" as well as causes when applicable (p. 104) over the course of data analysis and interpretation. In 1978, Glaser carefully presented procedures of becoming sensitive to Basic Social Processes (BSPs), which are present in some grounded theory research but not all. BSPs "are fundamental, patterned processes in the organization of social behaviors which occur over time and go on irrespective of the conditional variation of place" (p. 100) and to which

Glaser instructs researchers to be sensitive. Such instructions direct researchers to using pre-conceived categories and ideas. At the same time, they advise other researchers to maintain a sensitivity to all possible theoretical relevances" (p. 194). Strauss and Corbin (1990) further developed elaboration theory and also alerted researchers to the social ecologies of the phenomena they study. "Pre-conceived" ideas held lightly are sensitizing concepts, and without sensitizing concepts researchers have no way of making sense of their data. Strauss and Glaser (1970) made a similar point in their commentary on a case history of a woman dying of cancer in a hospital setting, among many other works.

Hypothesis Testing In Analytic Induction

Analytic induction goes beyond the use of sensitizing concepts and tests explicit hypotheses for the purpose of modifying hypotheses to fit data. Similar to the procedures of grounded theory, analytic induction begins with explicit hypotheses, and the goal is to modify these hypotheses to fit emerging understandings of the data (Gilgun, 1995b). Researchers using analytic induction have goals similar to those of grounded theorists: to develop relevant hypotheses that are modifiable, work, and fit the data. Lindesmith (1947) developed his hypothesis on opium addiction not from a literature review but from observations and conversations with addicts. He tested the hypothesis through interviewing more than 60 addicts, seeking to disconfirm the hypothesis so as to modify it to fit his emerging findings. Only after some ideas "crystallized" through these primarily inductive procedures did he consult previous research and theory. Lindesmith reviewed the theory many times over the course of the interviews, and this led him to conclude that the theory would be revised continuously in response to new information. Like those who came before him, therefore, Lindesmith discussed the open-ended nature of inductively-derived theory.

Methodologists such as Znaniecki (1934) support and amplify Lindesmith's conclusions about the nature of inductively-developed theory. Znaniecki wrote that the challenge in analytic induction is to find general principles that will guide the analysis and help identify the central features of cases. Centrality is not dependent upon how often it appears. Out of comparisons and general principles, researchers formulate hypotheses. Znaniecki (1934) saw contradictory evidence as reason to develop competing hypotheses and to continue the analysis out of which "emerges new hypotheses and new problems" (p. 282). Later methodologists have names for two of these processes: constant comparison (Glaser & Strauss, 1967) which was foreshadowed by Bott's use of the term and negative case analysis (Cressey, 1953, among others), which is a deliberate seeking out of cases that will disconfirm the emerging theory. Besides Lindesmith (1947)'s research, and there are a few other examples as well (Cressey, 1953; Becker, 1953; Gilgun, 1995b; Nosek et al, 1995; Olesen, Heading, Shadick, & Bistodeau, 1994).

Given the emphasis during these middle years on generalizability and the hope for theory that was universal and deterministically causal, it is not surprising that some researchers dismissed the hypotheses produced by inductive procedures. Manning (1982), for example, misinterpreted analytic induction, evaluating it in terms of its ability to produce universal, deterministically causal hypotheses and found it lacking in these regards, a view that Vidich and Lyman (1994) echoed. As the earlier discussion shows, a careful reading of the originators of inductive research processes illustrates that they did not intend analytic induction to produce such hypotheses. Rather, researcher after researcher, such as Bott (1957/1971), Lindesmith (1947), Znaniecki (1934), Thomas and Znaniecki (1918-1920/1927), and Glaser and Strauss (1967) stated that their hypotheses were situated, bounded by space, time, and persons, and that any relationships they discovered were tentative, subject to revision when held up to a new case. Such hypotheses illuminate other similar situations but were not presumed automatically to be generalizable to any other situation (Alasuutari, 1996; Gilgun, 1994a & b; Stake, 1996) Instead, these hypotheses were deliberately flexible in order to allow their application to particular settings. Furthermore, deterministic causality was not the style of causality in which they were interested, when if they were interested in causation at all. Rather they were interested in interactions between persons and environments and how larger social forces affected individuals and groups.

Applied Research and Inductive Methods

Glaser and Strauss (1967) unselfconsciously assumed that inductively-derived grounded theories sometimes would be used to ameliorate social conditions, a social reform orientation that harkens to the originators of qualitative family research, such as the pragmatist philosophers, as discussed earlier. Extending the principle of modifiability, they wrote that persons who want to apply grounded theories can "can bend, adjust or quickly reformulate" them when fitting them to "situational realities that he [sic] wishes to improve" (p. 242). They pointed out that nurses use grounded theories to guide their work with dying patients.

The assumption that grounded theory is flexible can be extended to any inductively-derived theory. Such perspectives invite clinical researchers such as nurses, social workers, family therapists, clinical psychologists, and psychiatrists to use inductive methods in their

41

research. This is exactly what began happening during these middle years as Strauss, Glaser, and Schatzman educated generations of nurses at the University of California, San Francisco. As will be discussed in the third section of this chapter, nursing researchers have been highly productive in furthering the development of inductive, qualitative research methods. Other clinical disciplines are becoming aware of the usefulness of these methods.

Credibility of Inductive Research

During these middle years, the epistemological concerns of reliability and validity were the standards by which the quality of research was judged. Though much of qualitative research is concerned with ontological issues, such as what it means to be human in particular situations, qualitative researchers could and sometimes did justify their research in the epistemological terms of their day (e.g., Jick, 1979; LeCompte & Goetz, 1982; Kidder, 1981; Rosenblatt, 1983). Most qualitative approaches, however, represented more than what could be accounted for in these other epistemologies.

Glaser and Strauss (1967) were concerned that qualitative research be taken seriously. Building on Chicago traditions, they developed guidelines for evaluating qualitative research that were quite different from the prevailing ideas of the time. As they pointed out, the immersion of researchers in the field became a fundamental argument for the strength of qualitative research. By the time researchers are ready to publish, they are so intimate with their material that they have great confidence in its credibility.

Researchers's confidence and the demonstration of credibility, however, are not the same thing, as Glaser and Strauss demonstrated. Researchers have the responsibility to convey the bases on which others may conclude that the findings are credible. They can do so in several ways. Credibility rests on conveying findings in understandable terms. The first strategy that Glaser and Strauss (1967) suggested is for researchers to present their theoretical frameworks using conventional "abstract social science terminology" (p. 228). The presentation should be extensive, and, since, the terms are familiar, the framework should be readily understood.

The second strategy that Glaser and Strauss (1967) discussed is to present findings in such ways that readers are "sufficiently caught up in the description so that he [sic] feels vicariously that he [sic] was also in the field" (p. 230). Glaser (1978) later called this quality "grab." This connects to the methodological stances of the Chicago School of Sociology, especially as represented by Robert Park and others. Denzin, who worked for several years with Lindesmith and Strauss (Lindesmith,

Strauss, & Denzin, 1975) on a social psychology textbook, reworked this idea for contemporary times and saw its relevance to policy research. He wrote, "*The perspectives and experiences of those persons who are served by applied programs must be grasped, interpreted, and understood, if solid, effective applied programs are to be created*" [emphasis in original text] (p. 12). A third strategy is to convey how researchers analyzed the data so that readers can understand how researchers arrived at their conclusions. Constantly comparing emerging findings across and within cases and searching for "negative cases" and "alternative hypotheses" (p. 230) all are important to delineate. Above all, integrating the theoretical statements with evidence help in conveying credibility.

Finally, Glaser and Strauss (1967) recognize the mutual responsibilities of researchers and their audiences. Researchers have the responsibility to convey findings as clearly as they can, including specifying how they arrived at their theoretical statements. Readers have the responsibility not only of demanding such evidence but also of making "the necessary corrections, adjustments, invalidations and inapplications when thinking about or using the theory" (p. 232). These researchers, therefore, made modest claims for their theories, seeing them as provisional and subject to interpretations and applications by others.

In *Theoretical Sensitivity*, Glaser (1978) again discussed the evaluation of grounded theory which he said is to be judged on fit, relevance, modifiability, and whether it works. Fit means whether or not abstract statements and concepts are congruent with the evidence. Refitting the theory to ever-emerging understandings as the research continues is part of the assessment. Thus, concepts and theory are not borrowed, but they "earn" their way into the emerging theory (p. 4). Findings become relevant when researchers allow emergence to happen and do not impose pre-conceived ideas onto them or do not shape findings to fit pre-formulations. Like other qualitative methodologists, such as Thomas and Znaniecki (1918/1920), discussed earlier, Glaser viewed all findings as modifiable as new understandings emerge. Modifiability, in fact, is a standard by which Glaser believes theory could fruitfully be evaluated. Theory that has fit, relevance, and modifiability, will also "work;" that is, "should be able to explain what happened, predict what will happen and interpret what is happening" (p. 4).

Guidelines for evaluating the theory generating by qualitative methods, then, were important to Glaser and to Strauss. Their views are based on grounded theory, which has much in common with others methods and methodologies, but there also are differences between approaches. These variations in approaches are to be taken into account if the many kinds of qualitative research is to be evaluated fairly. I will discuss some of these other guidelines for evaluation in the third section of this essay.

Other Influences on Qualitative Family Researchers

As important as analytic induction and the legacies of Strauss and Glaser may be, there are strands of qualitative family research that may not have been directly influenced by the Chicago School of Sociology. These include ethnomethodology (Holstein & Gubrium, 1994), critical theory (Comstock, 1982, Morrow, 1994; Lather, 1991; Osmond, 1987), qualitative family therapy research (Sprenkle & Moon, 1996), narrative theory (Bruner, 1990; Riessman, 1993; Rosenwald & Ochberg, 1992; Smith, 1993; Stivers, 1993), and some forms of feminist research (Reinharz, 1992). Many of the foundational ideas for these approaches to qualitative family research were developed during these middle years and are only now beginning to be actualized in qualitative family research. An exception is some feminist qualitative family research that is reminiscent of the Chicago School and flourished during these middle years in studies already cited (e.g.,Komarovsky, 1940, 1962; Lopata, 1971, 1973, 1979, 1984, 1985, 1992a, 1996; Rubin, 1976; Stack, 1974) and is flourishing today. These approaches to qualitative family research will be discussed in more detail in the third section of this essay.

A classic naturalistic study that has had a major influence on family therapy research is Kantor's and Lehr's (1975) analysis of family processes. This is one of the few data-based research projects where the qualitative methods used are named and delineated. They did participant observation with 19 families, aiming for as much detail as possible with a limited number of families. They used multiple qualitative methods for gathering data, including, besides participant observation, interviews, tape recording, videotapes, and self reports of thoughts, perceptions, and feelings of family members while they were engaged in behaviors observed by the researchers. They also used the Thematic Apperception Test. This qualitative study of the family resulted in a theory of family process which quickly was integrated into the theory and practice of family therapy. The concepts of open, closed, and random family types, and the family's use of space, time, and energy, and distance regulation models, all developed through qualitative methods, have become fundamental concepts in the understanding of families. The use of more than one method of data collection enhanced the quality of the findings. This study is a model study of qualitative research on families; it is a model because of its thoroughness, it use of multiple methods, and the quality and generativity of the theory it produced. This research is in the spirit of the Chicago School of Sociology.

The End of an Era and the Beginning of Another

I date the end of the middle years and the beginning of a new era as 1985 with the publication of LaRossa's and Wolf's (1985) "On Qualitative Family Research." This article is significant in the history of qualitative family research and may have signaled the influence of the postmodernist methodological pluralism that was emerging in other disciplines. After examining articles appearing in *Journal of Marriage and the Family* spanning almost 20 years (1965 to 1983), LaRossa and Wolf (1985) concluded that "qualitative family research is not taken seriously by [contemporary] family researchers," while, historically, they noted, it was "central" to the development of family studies (p. 538).

The article was a revision of a paper LaRossa and Wolf had presented the year before at the Pre-Conference Workshop on Theory Construction and Research Methodology at the National Council on Family Relations. The warm reception this paper received indicated the high interest qualitative methods holds for familiy scholars. Encouraged by such a reception, LaRossa founded the Qualitative Family Research Network, which meets yearly at NCFR conferences as a focus group of the Research and Theory Section. Interdisciplinary from the start, within seven years, the Network had about 400 members, with no advertising of its existence, but developing through word of mouth. Members keep in touch through a newsletter called *Qualitative Family Research*, through phone calls and letters, and, in the 1990s, through e-mail.

Encouraging each other and gaining in enthusiasm for their research goals and the methods that helped them to reach their goals, members planned symposia and paper presentations for the Pre-Conference Workshop and during the regular conference program. The book, *Qualitative Methods in Family Research*, which I edited with Kerry Daly and Gerald Handel (1992), was a project of the Network, financed with seed money from the Network and which to date receives a portion of the book's royalties.

There were other direct outcomes of LaRossa's and Wolf's (1985) article. LaRossa (1988) edited a special issue of *The Journal of Contemporary Ethnography* on qualitative family research, a collection of research reports based on observations, interviews, and written documents using a variety of perspectives. In his introductory article, LaRossa noted that Form (1987), editor of the *American Sociological Review*, had invited submissions of qualitative manuscripts and stated that they "would be taken seriously and given a fair review" (p. 243). Although, to date, few qualitative pieces appear in *ASR*, such a situation has many possible causes, including lack of training opportunities for both reviewers and reserachers, an underappreciation of research that emphasizes meaning, understanding, and lives experience, and the relatively small number of qualitative research projects as compared to positivistic, qualitative projects.

Demos (1990) followed up on LaRossa and Wolf's (1985) assessment of qualitative pieces and shifted perspectives to examine *JMF* from 1939 to 1987 for its studies of African-American families. He found what he labeled "underrepresentation of qualitative approaches" (p. 609), which reflected the overall under-representation of qualitative pieces in family journals. Coincidental or not with the scarcity of qualitative studies, Nye (1988) noted little use of theory in empirical research appearing in 50 years of *JMF*. As hopefully is evident, many forms of qualitative research have as its main purpose the generation of theory, and they use theory to guide research procedures.

Summary

During these middle years when qualitative methods were eclipsed by deductive, positivistic research based on probability theory and statistics, a relatively small group of sociologists, anthropologists, and methodologists carried on the traditions begun in the earlier part of the century at the University of Chicago. Not only did they produce work that is the foundation for many contemporary theories, but these researchers continued to develop the methods and methodologies that originated in the early years. They elaborated upon inductive methods, explicitly recognized the role of researchers' subjectivities and the centrality of the subjective aspects of informants' experiences, and were characteristically emancipatory in intent. Some, like Wax (1971) and Lindesmith (1947) became advocates for social causes as a result of their investigations.

Many were strong proponents of methodological pluralism, although some, like Handel, were puzzled by the relatively small scope of some of the quantitative research of his contemporaries. Many were explicitly devoted to the development of theory that fit data, that was relevant and modifiable, and that did what theory has some usefulness for explanation and prediction. Universalistic causal theory was not the goal of these researchers; rather they recognized the bounded nature of human understanding and often encouraged the modification of theory in order to fit and illuminate particular situations.

Glaser and Strauss (1967) are among the best-known methodologists to emerge from that period, possibly because they and their colleagues presented a way of analyzing qualitative data and of making theoretical sense of it. Other researchers, though less explicit about their methods and methodologies, continued to do inductive family research. During the middle years and earlier, like today, researchers must have access to procedures that help them to apply ideas to research projects. The work of Glaser and Strauss has been a major

46

source of guidance for contemporary qualitative family research. Had there been more wide-spread attention to the 1967 book and to Glaser's (1978) *Theoretical Sensitivity*, contemporary family theory would be much different. Glaser and Strauss built upon a long tradition stemming from and filtering through the Chicago School of Sociology.

Finally, when researchers such as LaRossa and Wolf (1985) pointed out the neglect of qualitative methods in family research, the responses of the scholarly community were strongly positive. Encouragement abounds. As I will show in the next section, training continues to lag but is gaining ground.

THE POSTMODERN PASTICHE

In our own day, the whirlwind of discussions on methodological, epistemological, ethical, and ontological aspects of research are harbingers that qualitative family research again is in the ascendence. Accompanying these spectacular philosophical and methodological changes is the on-going use of interviewing, observation, and document analysis that have been with us since the origins of sociological research, as discussed earlier. In fact, these methods and the procedures of data analysis and interpretation are the nuts and bolts of the doing of qualitative research. Ontologies, ethics, and epistemologies give directions, scope, and perspectives, but methods bring these philosophical issues to life.

The guiding principle for this section of this essay continues to be the centrality of the *doing* of qualitative research. Subjectivity, induction, and emancipation continue to be issues in contemporary qualitative research. Given the diversity of qualitative approaches now available, even within critical and interpretive paradigms (Schwandt, 1994), methodological pluralism is characteristic of contemporary times.

No More Ignorance About Philosophical
Underpinnings of Method

Today it is nearly impossible to remain naive about the philosophical and methodological underpinnings of the various qualitative research methods. There are far too many relevant texts raising our consciousness about ontologies, ethics, epistemologies, and methodologies for any researcher to ignore them. For example, the best-selling *Handbook of Qualitative Research* (Denzin & Lincoln, 1994) says practically nothing about research methods but bulges with chapters on ontologies, epistemologies, and methodologies relevant to qualitative research. Particularly compelling chapters for raising awareness of the philosophical contexts of contemporary qualitative research are Olesen's (1994) chapter on feminism, Guba & Lincoln (1994) on competing paradigms, Schwandt (1994) on constructivist, interpretivist approaches, and Holstein and Gubrium (1994) on ethnomethodology.

Other texts that are raising awareness include Dreyfus (1991) on Heidegerrian hermeneutics, Polkinghorne (1983) on methodologies for human sciences, and Harding (1987, 1991) and Fine (1992, 1994) on feminist methodologies and epistemologies, Lather (1991) on feminist postmodernism and critical theory, Baber and Allen (1992) on feminist postmodernism and families, Rosenau (1992) on postmodernism, and Morrow (1994) on the methodology of critical theory. Though focused on ethnography, the edited volume of Clifford and Marcus (1986), *Writing Culture*, has had a major trans-disciplinary influence, centered as it is on the writing of texts: who writes them, who and what the text represents, and the methods of writing. This is only a sampling of the outpouring of texts that challenge conventional thinking about approaches to research. Many others are noteworthy. A range of journals have had an impact on thinking about philosophical issues and will continue to do so. A few of them are *Signs, Symbolic Interactionism, Qualitative Health Research*, and *Qualitative Inquiry.*

Transformed forever, I hope, is the style of research training that avoided discussing the philosophical underpinnings of research methods and methodologies. There is far too much being written to allow such narrowness of vision. Hopefully today's students are learning the differences between induction and deduction, probabilistic and analytic generalizability, interpretive and positivistic research, critical emancipatory research and "pure" research. It is more likely now than ever that students are exposed to choices about how they might conduct their research. Given the current philosophical discussions, it may be routine a few years hence to ask Ph.D. students about the paradigms in which they are operating, not only when students are doing qualitative work, but when they also are doing large-scale surveys or experimental or quasi-experimental designs. Perhaps this will be routine in journal articles, books, and public and private presentations of research as well.

Disconnections

As significant as this outpouring of new ways to think about research may be, there is a serious downside. Researchers who do not already know something about the procedures of qualitative research can become confused about what to do with these generative ideas. Few of the above-cited texts and few journal articles link their philosophical discussions with specific procedures on how to do research. The connections between methods, methodologies, epistemologies, ethics, and ontologies, for many of today's researchers may be experienced as fragmented. The fragments are elusive, like flocks of butterflies. How explicitly to connect methods with ontologies, epistemologies and methodologies is a major challenge facing many of today's researchers.

Making sense of this unruly flock of terms related to qualitative methods is daunting. Some but certainly not all of the terms currently attached to styles of qualitative research include grounded theory, phenomenology, ethnography, ethnoscience, cultural studies, semiotics, discourse analysis, conversation analysis, analytic induction, social constructionism, constructivism, symbolic constructivism, interpretive phenomenology, interpretivism, feminist empiricism, deconstructionism, postmodernism, post-structuralism, post-positivism, constructivist, feminist standpointism, feminist postmodernism, hermeneutics, critical theory, reflexivity, participant observation, domain analysis, interpretive interactionism, sensitizing concepts, ethnomethodology, praxis, emancipation, constant comparative method, negative case analysis, theoretical sampling, axial coding, open coding, dimensional analysis, subjectivism, new objectivity, cultural analysis, hermeneutics, genealogy, methods, methodologies, ontologies, ethics, epistemologies, narrative analysis, *in vivo* codes, *in situ* codes, human sciences, historical realism, relativism, pragmatism, verstehen, meaning-making, positivism, induction, deduction, lived experience, paradigm cases. This is chaos. Chaos is a defining quality of postmodernism. Organizing and making sense of all these terms will take the lifetimes of several scholars.

Given time, effort, and study, this flock of terms possibly could be rounded up and organized under relatively few rubrics, such as post-positivism, social constructivism, and critical theory, three orientations to social research, or paradigms of social research. Social scientists Yvonna Lincoln and Egon Guba (Guba, 1990; Guba & Lincoln, 1994; Lincoln & Guba, 1985; Lincoln & Denzin, 1994) and feminist philosophers and methodologists (Baber & Allen, 1992; Harding, 1987; Fine, 1992, 1994; Lather, 1991; Thompson, 1992), among others, have popularized these terms and in so doing have taken leadership in discussing paradigm issues in social research. They have alerted research communities to the centrality of ontologies, epistemologies, ethics, and methodologies to social research.

Making the Connections: Interpretive Phenomenology

A few texts on qualitative family research are meeting the challenge of encompassing the intellectual contexts of the conduct of research; that is, they are successful in discussing method, methodologies, epistemologies, ethics, and ontologies. Exemplary in this regard is the

49

work of Benner (1994) and her students on interpretive phenomenology. Benner appears to have made the connections between her practical interest in promoting the health and well-being of nursing patients and the massive project of delineating not only a philosophical base for interpretive phenomenology but also the specific methods and methodologies that will actualize interpretive phenomenology.

Benner, who studied with Strauss, Glaser, and Schatzman and is a professor of nursing at the University of California, San Francisco, has developed an approach that is different from grounded theory (personal communication, 1992). Benner's interpretive phenomenology seeks to convey lived experience and what it means to be human, presented in research reports through straightforward categories and theoretical statements that are inductively derived. She sees interpretive phenomenology as a scholarly discipline that provides perspectives that can promote understanding of everyday practices and meanings. The research enterprises of such disciplines as nursing, clinical psychology, family therapy, and social work, guided by ethics of caring and responsiveness, may find philosophical homes in the ontologically-oriented interpretive phenomenology. Benner's students are beginning their research careers, and among them are qualitative family researchers SmithBattle (1993, 1994, 1995, 1996), Plager (1994), and Chesla (Chesla, 1994, 1995, Chesla, Martinson, & Muswaswes, 1994).

Lee SmithBattle's brief history of her career as a student summarizes a great deal of information about training in interpretive phenomenology, underlying principles, and their implications for the practice of this type of research:

I studied with Pat Benner (1994) at the University of California, San Francisco, School of Nursing. Pat had several classes on interpretive phenomenology. We had some classes where we read and discussed the philosophical background and issues of interpretive phenomenology, and we had other classes that were devoted to analysis of data. I as well as many of her other students had the opportunity to be research assistants on research she was conducting. These experiences were invaluable.

We also had quite a bit of course work at University of California at Berkeley with Hubert Dreyfus (1991) on early and late Heidegger, with Jane Rubin (1988) whose work on Kierkegaard was relevant to my work, and also with Martin Packer (Packer, 1985; Packer and Addison, 1989). So Pat's students had incredibly rich resources for studying the philosophical underpinnings of interpretive research and doing analysis as well.

Being an Interpretive Phenomenologist

I consider myself an interpretive phenomenologist (distinctive from Husserlian phenomenologists). Interpretive phenomenologists seek to understand lives, events, situations, or texts as lived out or as always situated by our concerns and by meanings available to us in the practices and social customs we learn by virtue of being members and participants of families, communities, nations, and epochs.

The point of interpretive work is to understand the lives, events, situations or texts that are studied, which requires understanding the background conditions and meanings that situate activities and contextualize the self. I particularly like Wax's (1971) definition of understanding:

Understanding...does not refer to a mysterious empathy between human beings. Nor does it refer to an intuitive or rationalistic ascription of motivations. Instead, it is a social phenomenon--a phenomenon of shared meanings. Thus, a fieldworker who approaches a strange people soon perceives that these people are saying and doing things which they understand but he does not understand. One of the strangers may make a particular gesture, whereupon all the other strangers laugh. They share in the understanding of what the gesture means, but the fieldworker does not. When he does share it, he beings to 'understand.' He possesses a part of the 'insider's' view" (p. 11).

Getting insiders' perspectives is what interpretive researchers strive for and is just as relevant to studying families, communities, practices (e.g. nursing, teaching, mothering, etc) or different epochs, as well as different cultures. So the goal is to understand people's lives or actions as they themselves understand their lives and actions, rather than imposing an "outsider" perspective which misconstrues and obscures.

SmithBattle's description of interpretive phenomenology shows its roots in human sciences traditions and thus its kinship with the origins of qualitative family research. What she does not say is that she is in a applied discipline and that the information she is gathering is not being done simply because it is interesting or because it contributes to theory, both of which are good reasons to do research and are true for hers. In her own case, she also has the goal of improving the lives of adolescent mothers, their children, and the mothers of the adolescent mothers. Within interpretive phenomenology, therefore, is an emancipatory thrust.

Discussions of the philosophical groundings of research methods in general and those used in family research in particular are so new that except for researchers trained in a particular paradigms, such as Benner's students in a type of interpretive phenomenology, most qualitative family researchers are inching our way toward more integrated research. Even the on-going use of the term *qualitative* in this essay

51

suggests that I and many of my contemporaries are equating styles of research with a term that designates the kind of data we gather. At some future time, the term *qualitative* may become outmoded and be replaced by other terms. Presently, the term *qualitative* has many possible meanings, such as interpretive, phenomenological, social constructivist, and, critical. Positivist qualitative research also is possible. The term *qualitative* may be here to stay because it is a blanket term that covers so many possible ways of doing research that involves language and that does not involve quantification.

On-going Elaborations of Qualitative Approaches

Benner's (1994) interpretive phenomenology is one of many examples of contemporary, on-going elaborations of qualitative approaches. Some of the other styles of research that family scholars currently are elaborations are grounded theory and analytic induction, ethnomethodology, feminist theory, critical theory, family therapy research, and textual analysis. These styles of research often are overlapping but each has its own distinctive qualities that contribute unique perspectives. Some are connected to Chicago Sociology while others are not. As Glaser (1978) stated more than two decades ago, we need all possible perspectives in our research quests.

Grounded Theory

Since the middle 1960s to the present, students of Glaser, Strauss, and Schatzman, among others, joined the effort to define grounded theory (e.g., Charmaz, 1975; 1990; Daly, 1995; Fagerhaugh, 1975; Gilgun, 1992b & d, 1994d; Quint, 1966, 1967; Reif, 1975; Stern, 1980, 1985; Strauss & Corbin, 1990; Wiener, 1975, among many others). Some responded to the perception of an under representation of "lived experience" (Wilson & Hutchinson, 1991), constructivist perspectives (Charmaz, 1990), and feminist perspectives (Wuest, 1995) in grounded theory and proposed modifications. Daly (1995) made the cogent point that although theory is the expected product of grounded theory research, a full accounting of the development of theory may require depicting the roles of researchers' selves in theory development. Grounded theory, then, is robust today, and is influencing the conduct of qualitative family research.

Scholarly journals publishing nursing research are particularly receptive to many forms of qualitative research, including grounded theory, while other disciplines apparently are lagging. From 1990 to 1995, for example, the data base CINAHL, which tracks nursing and allied health journals, logged a range of 74 to 106 articles using grounded theory methods. This represents a tripling of the number of articles using grounded theory during the 1980s. In contrast, Sociofile, a data base logging articles in sociologically-oriented journals, listed a range of 7 to 17 articles for each year of the 1990s. Some of the journals indexed in Sociofile also are indexed in CINAHL; the Sociofile numbers, then, are conflated with those of CINAHL. Sociologically-oriented disciplines, then, are lagging behind nursing researchers in their use of grounded theory methods.

Analytic Induction

Analytic induction, a form of qualitative analysis that is linked to and predates grounded theory, as the earlier discussion demonstrates, appears only rarely as a method of social research, possibly because it has been overshadowed by the work of Strauss and his colleagues on grounded theory (e.g., Glaser, 1992; Glaser & Strauss, 1967; Strauss, 1987; Strauss & Corbin, 1990, 1994). For example, during the 11 years between 1974 and 1995, Sociofile recorded 10 instances of the use of analytic induction as a method, and all but a few were on methodological issues and none were on family issues. This data base, however, did not record subsequently published contemporary uses of analytic induction of which I am aware. That is my article on incest perpetrators (Gilgun, 1995b) and the work of Rettig, Tam and Magistad (1996), who used a form of analytic induction in their study of justice principles in child support guidelines.

Transcendental Phenomenology

Moustakas (1990) explicated transcendental phenomenological research, based on Husserl's (1931, 1977) transcendental phenomenology. The three volumes of *The Duquense Studies in Phenomenological Psychology* (Volume 1 edited by Giorgi, Fischer, & von Eckartsberg, 1971; Volume 2, edited by Giorgi, Fischer, & Murray, 1975; and Volume 3, edited by Giorgi, Knowles, & Smith, 1979), contain a series of examples of this kind of research. As Smithbattle indicated above, practitioners of interpretive phenomenology see their work as quite different from transcendental phenomenology. According to Moustakas, transcendental phenomenology "emphasizes subjectivity" and seeks to discover "the essences of experience and provides a systematic and disciplined methodology for derivation of knowledge" (p. 45). "Transcendental" refers to the possibility of "a completely unbiased and presuppositionless state" (p. 60). Associated terms include intentionality, *noema, noesis, epoche,* bracketing, phenomenological reduction, imaginative variation, and textual-structural synthesis.

The process of doing transcendental phenomenological research involves in-depth interviewing as the primary method, analyzing data into clusters that have meanings in common, identification of variations on themes, portraying the themes through excerpts from the interviews, and creating a structural synthesis, which involves searching for the core meanings or essence of the experience (Patton, 1990). When the abstract terms of transcendental phenomenology are broken down into research operations, transcendental phenomenology has some procedures in common with both interpretive phenomenology and grounded theory. In regards to the claims of lack of bias and prior conceptualizations, Glaser (1978), however, would most likely remark, as he did in *Theoretical Sensitivity,* that "Immaculate conceptions are not necessary" (p. 8), a stance that has echoed over the ages among interpretive researchers. The term "transcendent," however, might appeal to Glaser, as he used it himself to describe how grounded theory transcends data.

Ethnomethodology

Ethnomethodology (Atkinson, 1988; Garfinkel, 1967) originated during the middle years and is achieving prominence today as a method of doing qualitative family research. Ethnomethodology's focus is on persons' interpretations of how they apply, bend, or disregard social values, rules, and sanctions in their explanations of their behaviors and decisions. According to Holstein and Gubrium (1994), the data of ethnomethodology is talk, or human discourse. Variable in terms of how ethnomethodology includes context in its analysis, the range is from ethnographic studies that look at the situated nature of discourse to forms of conversational analysis that often involves micro-analyses whose links to context may be unarticulated.

Garfinkel (1967), the originator of ethnomethodology, was termed "a renegade student" of Talcott Parsons by Lynch and Peyrot (1992, p. 113). Garfinkel developed ethnomethodology as an alternative to Parson's theory of social action. For Garfinkel, Parson's action theory was inadequate in that it assumed that human beings responded to "external forces" and were "motivated by internalized directives and imperatives" (Holstein & Gubrium, 1994, p. 264). Garfinkel, on the other hand, saw human beings as engaged in on-going interpretive processes, actively creating social institutions and the social order in particular contexts, a point similar to that of Strauss et al (1964) in their theory of negotiated order. Ethnomethodological researchers suspend "all commitments to an a priori or privileged version of social structure, focusing instead on how members accomplish, manage, and reproduce a *sense* [italics in original text] of social structure" (Holstein & Gubrium, 1994, p. 264). In sum, ethnomethodological research seeks to describe how human beings "account for the order in their everyday lives" (p. 264).

Gubrium and Holstein have taken the lead in applying enthomethodology to family discourse in a variety of settings, while Gale and Chenail have taken creative approaches to the study of family discourse in clinical settings. Among the studies of Gubrium and Holstein is the text *Where is Family?* (Gubrium & Holstein, 1990) which examines how family is enacted through language in a variety of organizational settings, such as nursing homes, caregiver support groups, and courtrooms. In a review article, they demonstrate in several ways how ethnomethodology can be applied to family discourse (Gubrium & Holstein, 1993). Gale analyzes the discourse of family therapy (Gale, 1991; Gale & Newfield, 1992), as does family therapist Chenail and his colleagues (Chenail, 1991; Chenail & Fortugno, 1995; Chenail et al, 1993; Chenail et al, 1990; Morris & Chenail, 1995).

Ethnomethodology does not appear to have a specific method of how to do research; it, instead, is more of methodology that includes a sketchy ontology and epistemology. Data are analyzed and interpreted through primarily inductive processes. The ideas of constructed realities and the centrality of processes of human interpretation appear to be driving principles in ethnomethodological research. Researchers within the ethnomethodological tradition are creating methods that are consistent with the philosophical principles of ethnomethodology.

Feminist Methodologies

Feminist qualitative family research, like interpretive phenomenology and ethnomethodology, is undergoing rapid development in contemporary times. Underpinning contemporary discussions are generative ideas present in articles published in feminist journals founded during the middle years--such as *Signs, Feminist Studies, Gender & Society, Psychology of Women Quarterly,* and *Women's Studies International Quarterly*--and major feminist books such as Bernard (1981), Blier (1984), Chodorow (1978), Dobash and Dobash (1979), Gilligan (1982), Hochschild (1983), hooks (1981, 1984), Komarovsky (1940, 1962), Lipman-Blumer (1984), Oakley (1974), Rossi and Calderwood (1973), Stanley & Wise (1983), and Thorne and Yalom (1982). These writings focus on the meanings of gender and its relationship to power, seek the points of view of women, and intend that their research be emancipatory, that is, to change social conditions, so that women can participate more fully in social life. Fine pointed out that many of today's feminist researchers attempt to avoid a stance of dominance toward informants, and she elaborated upon the challenges, contradictions, and compromises involved in doing so.

Feminist research is part of a reformist tradition, and many feminist researchers claim Jane Addams as their forbear (Deegan, 1990). Feminist social work researchers also claim reformists Edith Abbott and Sophinisba Breckinridge (Abbott, 1910, 1950; Abbott & Breckinridge, 1916), who were associates of Jane Addams and whose work was in the Chicago style. The origins of feminism and an on-going source of its energy and vision are reformist working at grass-roots levels on behalf of women and social change.

There is a considerable range of thought on which methods might best fit a feminist agenda (Osmond & Thorne, 1993; Reinharz, 1992; Thompson, 1992). Like ethnomethodology, feminist methodologies do not have a specific set of procedures for data collection and interpretation, and, the general consensus is that there is nothing inherently feminist about method; rather, researchers' ontologies, epistemologies, and methodologies create the *feminism* in feminist research. Feminist research enjoys methodological pluralism, although feminist postmodernism (Baber & Allen, 1992) most likely will be articulated in research methods that are flexible, allow researchers to be in close contact with informants, and permit analyses that show the intersection of individual lives and cultural themes and practices. Reflexivity is a major issue in contemporary feminist qualitative family research (Gilgun, 1995b; Hall & Zvonkovic, 1996; Sollie & Leslie, 1994; Stacey, 1990). Many feminist researchers situate themselves within a critical theory perspective (c.f, Fine, 1988, 1992, 1994; Lather, 1991).

Though contemporary journals that are not specifically feminist, such as *Journal of Marriage and the Family*, have published some qualitative feminist research (e.g., Blaisure & Allen, 1995; Gilgun, 1995b), feminist journals, such as *Gender & Society*, have offered space to many contemporary examples of qualitative feminist family research. Typical recent issues contain two or more qualitative pieces out of an average of five featured articles. Some of the more recent articles include topics such as men in child care (Murray, 1996), meanings of child care (Uttal, 1996), and women's multiple work strategies (Wright, 1995). The collection I edited with Marvin Sussman (Gilgun & Sussman, 1996) contains several different types of feminist qualitative family research, including Walker's (1996) interpretive study of letters 18 women wrote to each other annually for 25 years. The stories in these letters connect the private and public worlds; they communicate the events experienced, things hoped for, and things not done. Other feminist reports in the collection include Farnsworth's (1996) reflexive account of maternal bereavement, Holbrook's (1996) emancipatory study of the journal of a welfare mother, Hall and Zvonkovic (1996) on the effects of research on researchers, Hanawalt (1996) on a composite biography of a woman in medieval London, and Olsen's (1996) interviews of middle-class African-American adolescent young women.

Contemporary book-length qualitative feminist research receives wide recognition. For example, Martha McMahon's (1995) study of women's perspectives on engendering motherhood recently won two awards: one from the National Council on Family Relations and the other from the Sex and Gender Section of the American Sociological Association. Judith Stacey's (1990) work on late twentieth century families is foundational in contemporary feminist family studies. Feminist research based on numbers and statistical analysis not only can be done but is important to be done (c.f., Reinharz, 1992). In the future, however, it is highly likely that we will see an exponential increase in the numbers of feminist studies using qualitative methods.

Critical Theory

Critical theory originated in the early decades of this century and is developing rapidly today. The analysis of social power and the necessity of social change are core ideas in critical theory (Morrow, 1994; Osmond, 1987). Not only can feminism, with its focus on gender, power, and social change, be linked to critical theory (Lather, 1991; Osmond & Thorne, 1993), but so can social work with its core idea of social change.

The practitioners of critical theory seek both to understand and to change social conditions, and they specifically analyze structures and processes of social power from the points of view of those who are oppressed (Comstock, 1982; Lather, 1991; Morgaine, 1992a, 1994; Morrow, 1994). Robert Park might have approved some of the tenets of the unabashedly reformist critical theory. Park, as discussed earlier, criticized "do-gooders" for their paternalism, but he sought to understand persons in situations from their points of view and he saw knowledge as the pathway to human liberation.

Critical theorists attempt to be on the same plane as oppressed individuals, and, through dialogue, in the words of Morrow (1994), to "construct a coherent account of the understandings" individuals have of "their world" (p. 380). Dialogue also plays a part in the action-oriented aspects of critical theory, where critical theorists educate individuals about the social conditions under which they live. Social reform comes not from critical theorists but from the actions of oppressed persons (Morgaine, 1994).

The origins of critical theory is associated with the Frankfurt

Institute for Social Research, founded in 1923. Nine years later Hitler forced its theorists into exile. While contemporary critical theory claims a wide range of roots, from neo-Weberian conflict theory to neo-Marxist theory, critical theory is Marxist in origin (Morrow, 1994). In the 1960s and 1970s, influenced by Weber, phenomenology, and hermeneutics, Habermas (1971) and Giddens (1971)--neither of whom consider themselves within a Marxian tradition--revised critical theory (Morrow, 1994, p. 110). Reflexivity--that is, reflection--on social forces, ideologies, and institutions that are oppressive is a fundamental idea in critical methodology and fits well with phenomenological methodologies as they are discussed today.

Dollard's (1927) reflections on his experience researching for *Caste and Class in a Southern Town* is a precursor of the type of reflexivity that is part of critical theory's method. Osmond (1987) cited Lasch (1971), Zaretsky (1976) Donzelot (1977), the Red Collective (1978), Gordon (1977), Barry (1979), Carmody (1979) Laws (1979), Janeway (1980) as examples of critical theory. For the most part, these researchers depended a great deal on interviews, document analysis, and reflections on the social order.

The influence of critical theory in contemporary qualitative family research is in its beginning stages, appearing, for example, in Fine's (1988) evaluation of a sex education program and in the work of Morgaine (1992a, 1992b, 1994) on family life education. Osmond (1987), as discussed earlier, critiqued family studies for its normative focus and offers radical-critical theory as a road map toward looking at all aspects of family life in terms of power relations, both within the family and between the family and other social institutions.

The research methods of critical theory are largely undelineated, with Barton (1971), Comstock (1982), Eichler (1981), Morgaine (1994), and Morrow (1994) offering some guidance. Morrow stated that methods most strongly associated with critical theory involves comparative analysis, the application of general theories of history, and the "analysis of causal regularities" (p. 253). Comparative analyses of a small number of cases in contrast to large samples analyzed through statistics is emerging as an approach compatible with critical theory.

Morgaine (1994) used reflective, critical inquiry (Comstock, 1982; Friere 1968/1986; Lather, 1991) as a method of developing a theory of self-formation. A method that involves inquiring into and reflecting upon the situations of others and of the self, critical inquiry as Morgaine practiced it followed Comstock's recommendations for the procedures of the research. The first step is the identification of an oppressed group or a group whose self-interest was being undercut by their own ideologies. In Morgaine's case, the group of interest were her own students, and her focus was their ideologies, which she viewed as interfering with their effectiveness in working with children and families. The second step is developing an understanding of the circumstances and perspectives of the group chosen. Dialogue and on-going reflection on all aspects of the engagement with subjects characterize the process. Through reflection and dialogue, the critical theorist begins to identify emergent themes, and then examines the historical context of these themes, which is the third step. In Morgaine's study, she found power and saving face to be major themes among her students, and she consequently read widely about social power and subordination. Still following Comstock, she took the fourth step of creating an explanation for the belief systems of her students. Finally, she offered the explanations to her students, who began to change their views of themselves. Morgaine's identification of themes is similar to procedures in grounded theory analysis (Glaser & Strauss, 1967; Strauss, 1987; Strauss & Corbin, 1990).

Qualitative methods that seek insider perspectives are well-suited to critical research, especially interviews, in light on the emphasis on dialogue. Document analysis, observation, and critical reflection are other methods that further the goals of critical theory. The *critical* in critical research comes from its philosophical base: methods actualize the ideas, and the same methods can be used in other types of research whose purposes are quite different from those of critical theory.

Family Therapy

Qualitative methods are the unacknowledged underpinnings of theory development in family therapy. The theoretical foundation of contemporary family therapy is based on the formulations of gifted therapists who were in direct interaction with clients. A look at the writings of some of the major family therapy theorists, however, shows they did not discuss how they arrived at their formulations. Given the nature of the practice of family therapy, it is safe to state that these therapists developed their theories through participant observation, often supplemented by audiotapes and videotapes. What kind of observation, how long, how many families, and how data are collected and analyzed remained unstated and, undoubtedly, were not recorded systematically.

Several contemporary researchers have noted the congruence of many family therapy theories with methodologies associated with qualitative research (e.g., Gilgun, 1990b; Moon, Dillon, & Sprenkle, 1990; Sells, Smith, & Sprenkle, 1995). Though originating from many theoretical and methodological roots (Newmark & Beels, 1994), much of the theory of family therapy broadly is based on the work of anthropologist Gregory Bateson (1972) and systems theorist Bertalanffy (1968). Notions such as the significance of context, notions of circular causality, the non-existence of reality independent of the observer, and the reciprocal relationship of client and therapist (Gurman, Kniskern, and Pinsof, 1986) characterize family therapy.

This congruence is widely recognized and is likely to result in a great increase in the use of qualitative methods for research on family therapy. Doherty (this volume) pointed out that not only did family therapy move toward postmodernism in the late 1980s, leading to an open field in terms of how to conduct qualitative family therapy research. To provide another perspective on contemporary qualitative family therapy, I invited Cynthia Franklin (Franklin, 1996a, 1996b, 1995; Franklin & Jordan, 1995), a family therapist and an associate professor of social work at the University of Texas at Austin, to write a short overview. This is what she wrote:

The field of family therapy has endorsed both qualitative and quantitative methods of research. In the past decade, family therapy researchers have increasingly called for an acceptance of qualitative research as well as an integration of qualitative and quantitative methods (Moon et al, 1990; Sells et al, 1995; Sprenkle & Bischoff, 1995). Half of a recent textbook on family therapy research (Sprenkle & Moon, 1996) is devoted to qualitative methods, although there are only a few examples of how it actually is done.

Studies using qualitative methods are appearing in greater frequency in family therapy literature, and the approaches are diverse, including ethnographies (e.g. Newfield, Kuehl, Joanning, & Quinn, 1990; Sells, Smith, Coe, Yoshioka & Robbins, 1994; Smith, Winston & Yoshioka, 1992; Smith, Yoshioka, & Winston, 1993; Smith, Sells, & Clevenger, 1994), discourse and conversation analysis borrowing from ethnomethodology (e.g. Buttny, 1990; Buttny & Jenson, 1995; Chenail & Fortugno, 1995; Gale & Newfield, 1992; Todtman, 1995), case studies using dialectical analysis (e.g. Franklin, 1996; Keeney & Ross, 1985), Recursive Frame Analysis (e.g. Keeney, 1990; Keeney & Bobele, 1989), focus groups (e.g. Polson & Piercy, 1993), and phenomenology (Pollner & McDonald-Wilker, 1985, Stamp, 1991).

Many family therapy researchers draw from a wide range of methodologies, epistemologies, and ontologies. Typical of this trend is the research of Newfield et al (1990) who used ethnographic interviews (Spradley, 1979) to explore the perceptions of adolescent clients who participated in systemic family therapy in the context of substance abuse treatment. Systemic family therapies propose that reciprocity between therapists and clients is key to the therapy process. Attention to feedback from clients, however, is a neglected aspect of research on family therapy. The researchers based their interpretations on postmodern anthropology and radical constructivism, both of which consider "reality" more imagined than real. The scientist who believes he/she is objective actually confuses his/her own perceptions with what the client "really" feels.

Another recent development is the growth of family therapy educational programs that emphasize qualitative research methods. Most programs teach qualitative as well as quantitative research, and some programs specialize in qualitative methods. Nova Southeastern University in Florida and University of Iowa, for example, have research programs that prepare their Ph.D. students to be qualitative researchers.

Family therapy by its nature is applied and it can be considered emancipatory in that it seeks to liberate persons from oppressive patterns of interaction. Within family therapy research, there is recognition of subjectivist, constructivist dimensions of the experiences of both clients and practitioners, and the research often is based on inductive methods.

The Analysis of Texts

Much of the work currently being done in qualitative family research can be viewed as forms of textual analysis, a term associated with postmodernism. In the broadest sense, all qualitative research is an analysis of texts, when texts are defined as they usually are in postmodern writing; that is, as anything that can be interpreted, such as clothing, the fins of cars, cathedrals, radio towers, and mass media such as television, computer games, and radio programs (Barthes, 1974; Fiske, 1994; Gilgun, 1995a; Manning & Callum-Swan, 1994; Noth, 1995). In general, however, textual analysis usually refers to studies of various types of written texts in order to deconstruct their significance. Synonyms for deconstruction include "unpacking" and "decoding;" that is, the breaking down of texts to explore meanings, contradictions, connotations, relationships of images and connotations to culture.

This inclusive definition is applicable to most forms of textual analysis, and there appear to be unlimited numbers of ways to analyze texts. I think of textual analysis as a huge and open field, strewn with countless tools, objects, and other materials, metaphors for the plethora of methods, methodologies, epistemologies, and ontologies now available to researchers, as discussed earlier. Researchers can chose among these items and use them to construct their particular ways of conducting analyses of texts. For example, when talk comprises the text, then the method can be termed *discourse analysis*. Enthnomethodology, discussed earlier is a form of discourse analysis. Textual analysis can be termed *narrative analysis* when the data can be construed as composed of a story or story line. Cultural studies (Alasuutari, 1996; Denzin, 1995; Fiske, 1994; Schwartz, 1994) is another form of textual analysis that looks for persons' enactments of cultural themes and practices in particular settings and times.

There are a myriad of other choices within textual analysis. The purposes of textual analysis can be multiple, such as human emancipation, or expository so as to inform, or to create new understandings through formulation of concepts and theories. In addition, researchers can chose from a range of ways to use concepts and theory in the analysis: the use of codes formulated by others (Barthes, 1974), grounded theory, analytic induction, and phenomenology. Researchers can share their responses to the text and disclose their relationships to informants; or they may not. Some examples of family research that is unabashedly reflexive, that uses principles from cultural analysis, and are based on narrative accounts is Steedman's (1991) biography of Margaret McMillan, a pioneer in nursery education, and Hamabata's (1993) reflexive, postmodern ethnography of wealthy Japanese families.

Understandably, practitioners generally avoid defining textual analysis, possibly because of the range of types and the overlapping and amorphous boundaries of types. For instance, researchers can do a discourse analysis of a story that involves linking the particularities of the story to wider cultural themes and practices. This at once is narrative, discourse, and cultural analyses. If researchers break the text into units and then analyze the units for the connotations of words and particularizations of the wider culture, this can be considered a narrative, semiotic, deconstructionist, postmodern discourse analysis. Finally, if the researcher's purpose is to bring about some kind of social reform, then *emancipatory* is yet another term that can accurately describe some aspects of the research.

Textual analysis, like feminist research, critical theory, and ethnomethodology, can be infused with many combinations of methodologies, epistemologies, and ontologies. The *textuality* of a piece of research arises from the perspectives researchers impose on their subject matter.

Narrative analysis. Narrative analysis is increasingly discussed in the social sciences; it also is receiving a great deal of attention as an approach to family therapy (Freedman & Combs, 1996; Gilligan & Price, 1993; White & Epston, 1990), but less so as a form of family therapy research. Story is the central metaphor in narrative theory, but the approach is composed of diverse traditions, from the near atheoretical and practical approaches of oral histories, to the methodologically dense discussions in feminist writings (Smith, 1993; Stivers, 1993), to the constructivist versions of psychologists and philosophers (Bruner, 1990; McCabe & Peterson, 1991; Manning & Cullum-Swan, 1994; Mischler, 1993; Singer & Salovey, 1993), and the social constructivist, emancipatory versions of Riessmann (1990, 1993, 1994) and McLaughlin and Tierney (1993).

Martin's (1995) oral history project on African-American families of the rural south provides an example of applications of narrative analysis to the understanding of family life over time. Oral history in particular, but other many forms of narrative research as well, offer opportunities to give voice to the "voiceless," that is, to persons whose experiences and interests are not well-represented in social science, such as poor rural African-Americans or women with HIV/AIDS. Some researchers who are proponents of narrative analysis are frankly emancipatory in intent. LeCompte (1993), for instance, stated that giving voice to the voiceless is important because silenced persons provide views that are "counter-hegemonic" (p. 10). Emancipation in narrative research can be personal as well. Jago's (1996) personal account of her father's abandonment, in her words, "helped me confront my personal demons and transform my family story" (p. 514), although she also demonstrated the methodological point of how stories can be revised over time.

The semiotic, post-structuralist analytic approach of Roland Barthes (1974), whose method I replicated in a study of family murder (Gilgun, 1995a), discussed earlier, is a form of narrative analysis, where the text is broken and deconstructed. Semiotics, a form of textual analysis, is a study of signs and what signs signify. Signs constitute texts of whatever sort. I chose the written text that I analyzed from transcripts of several months worth of interviewing. I guided my choice of text partially by how the pieces of a man's account contributed to the temporal, narrative flow of a story, with a beginning, middle, and end. Barthes' five codes, which provide a fluid structure to the analysis, guided me toward an analysis of how culture and individual behavior and experience intersect, on the connotations of language, and on the bounded actions of narrators. Semiotics, however, ranges far more widely than written texts and includes the study of anything that can be interpreted, including the fins of cars, paintings, and music (Noth, 1995). Narrative analysis, then, like textual analysis more generally, can be created in any number of guises, depending upon the researchers' philosophical and methodological approaches.

Cultural studies. The focus of cultural studies is on how persons perform or enact particularized cultural themes and practices (Denzin, 1995). Human beings are assumed to have various degrees of agency. An additional assumption is that the particularized meanings are ever-shifting and conflictual (Fiske, 1994). Fiske, along with some others, views the term *cultural studies* as "contested and currently trendy" (p. 189) and do not define it. Although there are many styles of doing cultural studies (Schwartz, 1994), practitioners generally view human beings as not passive recipients of culture but as persons who actively shape, interpret, give meaning to, repress, and transcend their experiences and socialization. Texts that contain stories are the usual focus of analysis. Theory can be but is not necessarily a product of cultural studies (Alasuutari, 1996). Conceptual frameworks associated with cultural studies include feminist post-structuralism, neo-Marxism, feminist materialism (Bogdan & Biklen, 1992), and interpretive cultural studies (Denzin, 1995). Thus interest could be in power--who has it and how it manifests itself--and in the meanings persons draw from other persons, emotions, acts, consequences, and objects.

Families as depicted in the media have been subjects of cultural studies. Fiske (1994), for example, "told a story" about the television show "Married...With Children" and located his analysis within such considerations as "the market economy," "New information technologies," and the depiction of teenagers in the media (p. 190). Fiske linked the specifics of the television show to cultural themes and practices, within a type of critical, emancipatory perspective. Denzin's (1995) version of cultural studies includes the analysis of the meanings of films and the search for "storied" lives.

Ethnography. Cultural studies and ethnographies have an interest in culture, but anthropological ethnographies have come under severe criticism, considered by some to be products of a colonial mentality where ethnographers view informants as the Other and where researchers think of themselves as neutral, when in fact they have standpoints conditioned by gender, race, class, nationality, and self-interest (Clifford & Marcus, 1986; Fine, 1994). Those who practice cultural studies want to divest themselves of such baggage, and there is an effort in ethnographies to do so as well. Writing is a major concern for contemporary ethnographers, sparked by the work represented in Clifford and other postmodern efforts. The subtitle of Clifford's and Marcus's book is "The Poetics and Politics of Ethnography," terms that suggest both the literary nature and the interest in power dynamics in personal/cultural intersections.

Recently, *Journal of Contemporary Ethnography* and *Symbolic Interactionism* have given considerable attention to examining the possibilities for ethnography, which has been challenged by "postmodernist and poststructuralist perspectives on truth, neutrality, objectivity, and language" (Bochner & Ellis, 1996, p. 3). Mitchell and Charmaz (1996) provide a enlightening dialogue that shows some of the implications for ethnography of the postmodern emphasis on writing. Some examples of contemporary experimental ethnographies that connect to family studies are Ellis's (1995) *Final Negotiations* and Brown's (1996) study of a Jewish family resort area. The intersections of feminism, cultural studies, ethnography, autobiography, and

64

postcolonialism is the topic of a recent book by Visweswaran (1994). Methodological discussions of feminist ethnographies (Reinharz, 1992) have many generative ideas for the conduct of research that is continually reflexive about the meanings of gender and power in a wide range of social contexts.

There also continue to be less "postmodernist" trends in ethnography. For instance, Lofland and Lofland (1995) have published their third edition of *Analyzing Social Settings* to critical acclaim (Charmaz & Preissle, 1996), primarily for its accessibility to beginning researchers. The terms *ethnography* and *ethnographic* travel across disciplines; they are widely used, being found, among other places, in some ethnomethodological studies and in family therapy research. Like any other kind of qualitative family research, ethnographic family research is an open field.

Rich Tradition of Book-Length Studies

These postmodern times have opened unprecedented opportunities for the deployment and development of qualitative research methods. Researchers can pick and chose among ontologies, epistemologies, methodologies, and methods. Pluralism applies not only to qualitative approaches but to any number of mathematically-based approaches as well. Despite these developments within family research and in the larger context provided by contemporary discussions, overall there still are few articles on qualitative family research compared to quantitative reports. Ambert, Adler, Adler, and Detzner (1995) pointed out that four of 527 articles published in *Journal of Marriage and the Family*, between 1989 to 1994 were entirely qualitative: in addition, one was partly qualitative and five others used a combination of qualitative and quantitative approaches, for a total of 1.9%.

The rarity of journal articles contrasts with a tradition of qualitative family research being published in books, which often use a variety of sources of data and whose authors are trained in a variety of disciplines, as Rosenblatt's and Fischer's (1993) review of qualitative family research demonstrates. Among the classics Rosenblatt and Fischer cited are Bossard's and Boll's (1950) study of family ritual, Waller's (1930) case studies of divorce, Hunt (1969) on marital infidelity, and Rainwater's (1970) study of families in federal housing projects. These books generally are esteemed in family studies.

Today, book-length studies based on historical documents are fairly easy to find, and they include historian Barbara Hanawalt's (1986, 1993) studies of medieval families, social psychologist Paul Rosenblatt's (1983) analysis of nineteenth century diaries and twentieth century grief theories, historian Drew Gilpin Faust's (1996) study of women in the slaveholding Southern states during the American Civil War, ethnographer Hamabata's (1993) study of Japanese business families, Curry's (1996) account of a southern African American family's courage in creating opportunities for the children's education, and social worker Howard Goldstein's (1996) study of the life course of Jewish children who grew up in an orphanage from the 1920s to the 1940s. The interdisciplinary team of Patricia Bell-Scott, Beverly Guy-Sheftall, Jacqueline Jones Royster, Janet Sims-Wood, Miriam DeCosta-Willis, & Lucie Fultz (1991) assembled a major collection of documents portraying mother-daughter relationships in black families.

Book-length studies based on interviews and observations often win wide recognition. As mentioned earlier, Martha McMahon's (1995) book has won two awards. The last three books, including McMahon's, that received the Student/New Professional Book Award sponsored by the National Council on Family Relations and Sage Publications, were based on qualitative methods (e.g., Dienhart [in press] and Nadeau [in press]).

Encouragement Abounds

Like other editorial boards, *Journal of Marriage and the Family* editors and commentators during the last few decades have been favorable to qualitative family research. Wiseman (1981) predicted family researchers "will move toward qualitative, naturalistic approaches," given what she saw as a "burgeoning interest" in micro-interactions within families (p. 264). In the same issue, Hill (1981) discussed the projected limited resources for social science research and predicted that researchers may do more exploratory and descriptive studies, which generate "more discoveries per hour expended than large scale quantitative verification or experimentally designed studies in laboratories" (p. 256). The next year, Sprey (1982), as editor of *JMF*, said he would like to see more qualitative articles in the journal. Marilyn Coleman, editor from 1990 to 1995, encouraged the submission of articles based on qualitative methods. *Family Relations*, the applied journal of the National Council on Family Relations, *Families in Society*, published by Family Service America, and Journal of Family Issues, have also displayed an openness to qualitative family research, as have other journals, less strongly associated with family studies, including *Qualitative Inquiry, Qualitative Sociology*, and *Journal of Contemporary Ethnography*. For several decades, then, editors and other gatekeepers hardly could have been more encouraging.

Learning to be a Qualitative Researcher

Though not a lot has changed in terms of quantities of qualitative family research published in scholarly journals since LaRossa and Wolf (1985) published their essay, the intellectual context has been transformed, as the earlier discussion demonstrated. The lag between intellectual context, encouragement, and actual publications likely is due to many factors. Lack of training in qualitative methods is a primary reason. Not only does the quality of research suffer because of lack of training, but often the quality of the reviews of manuscripts is compromised by undertrained reviewers. Among the many reviewer-related issues that Ambert et al (1995) identified are bias against the so-called "softness" of qualitative research, an insistence upon documentation of qualitative work when such documentation is not required in quantitative approaches, the epistemologic-specific training of some qualitative researchers who are unable to appreciate ways of qualitative research that run counter to their own training,and a lack of appreciation of research that seeks to raise new questions rather than formulate new theory.

Lack of training shows itself in the quality of some of the manuscripts submitted for publication. Marilyn Coleman, former editor of *Journal of Marriage and the Family,* found that reviewers who were qualitative researchers often rejected manuscripts as not good examples of qualitative research. She and the reviewers often worked with authors through revision after revision in order to get a piece in shape for publication (Coleman, personal communication, 1996). In co-editing two volumes of qualitative family research (Gilgun et al, 1992; Gilgun & Sussman, 1996) and in reading manuscripts for several journals, I found that some researchers could analyze and write up their material in exemplary ways, but others needed much editorial guidance, not because they were unintelligent but because they simply did not know how to do it.

Though there now is more training than ever before now available, there are few programs whose primary emphasis is on qualitative approaches. Higher education rarely offers students the in-depth training that competency in these methods requires. Those who want to learn how to do qualitative analysis and who do not have teachers readily available--and their numbers are not known--learn by trial and error, a difficult route, since most texts are sketchy about procedures of data analysis (Strauss, 1987; Schatzman, 1991).

Ralph LaRossa (LaRossa, 1983; LaRossa & LaRossa 1981) tells a story that stands for the experiences of many contemporary qualitative researchers. He described how he learned to do qualitative analysis when he was a Ph.D. student in sociology at the University of New Hampshire: "I did what Richard Gelles (1974) had done two years before me. I had my interviews transcribed. I read them several times. I cut them up in strips. I wrote memos. Then I got to the point where I wanted to know what to do next. I put the piles on the floor next to me, and I read the chapter in Glaser and Strauss (1967) on the constant comparative method. They told me I was supposed to look for concepts" (Gilgun, 1993a, pp. 6-7). Opportunities to learn how to do qualitative analysis, then, have been limited in the past and, though more available now, rarely is available in the depth required for competency.

Training Through Seminars

One of the few opportunities for intensive academic training in qualitative methods has been at the University of California, San Francisco. As discussed earlier, with the arrival of Strauss in the late 1960s to found the department of social and behavioral sciences, nursing doctoral students for decades took a sequence of research courses that Strauss, Schatzman, and Glaser taught. They also took philosophy of science courses at the University of California, Berkeley. Not only did many of these graduates go on to teach qualitative methods at other schools of nursing, but other nursing research professors taught additional forms of qualitative research, such as Newman's method of understanding health as expanding consciousness (Newman, 1986, 1989; Lamendola & Newman, 1994) and transcultural nursing and ethnoscience (Leininger, 1969, 1978, 1985). As a result, nursing qualitative research is more advanced than the research of most other disciplines.

Learning how to do qualitative research can involve years of training in interactive seminars, based on group analysis of data. These seminars appear to be the most effective way to learn (Gilgun, 1992b & c; Schatzman, 1991; Strauss, 1987; Strauss & Corbin, 1990). Traditional in qualitative research, group analysis of data for teaching purposes were used by Robert Park, Ernest Burgess, and Vivian Palmer at the University of Chicago during the 20s and early 30s (Bulmer, 1984) and were similar to the group data analysis sessions that Booth conducted when he did studies of the London poor (Webb & Webb, 1932). A contemporary example of this approach to data analysis is described in Olesen, Droes, Hatton, Chico, and Schatzman, (1994). In seminars, the usual method is for students to provide copies of their fieldnotes a week or so ahead of time to other seminar participants. Each week participants discuss fieldnotes in detail. Beginning researchers learn analysis through doing it, an action-oriented approach that may have received some of its rationale from Dewey (1922, 1938), whose ideas were highly influential at the University of Chicago earlier in this century, as discussed earlier.

Syracuse University is another locale where in-depth training in qualitative methods has been available for more than 30 years. Bogdan

(Gilgun, 1992c) provided a sense of what it was like for him to be a student in the 1960s in a seminar with Blanche Geer (Becker Geer, & Hughes, 1968; Becker, Geer, Hughes, & Strauss, 1961):

In the seminar, we talked about what was happening in our own studies. A lot of it was sharing stories and problems. There was no text book. I recall there were no readings, except that Blanche would refer you to things you could read to help illuminate some problem or some conceptual area she thought your study was about. We were required to do an observation with a corresponding set of notes each week. It was a lot of work. I really got into it. Part of the enjoyment was feeling and working in a way I had never worked before. I like what the process produced. I arranged my week so I could do the work for the seminar (p. 9).

Though some students thrived in these seminars, others were not so responsive. Susan O'Connor, writing of her doctoral research training at Syracuse University in the 1990s, showed how she and several of her student colleagues were taken by the methods, while other students were repelled by their ambiguity:

My formal exposure to qualitative methods was a first semester course in the Ph.D. program. This was a year-long research methodology course. The first six weeks were devoted to qualitative research. Sari Knopp Biklen (Bodgan & Biklen, 1992) was our instructor. She was strong and clear about the method and her dissemination of information. We were immediately required to begin our research. I remember thinking that I didn't have enough knowledge of the process and had so many questions that should be answered. I came to find rather quickly that this was the nature of the research and that my learning was a process as well as a product.

The most striking memory I have from that class was how we as students separated ourselves out. There were those students who just did not connect with the process. It was too unclear. Those unknowns, I began learning, was what I loved and what connoted the difference between the paradigms. I understood what Sari was explaining, and I liked and understood the ambiguity, the inquiry, the discovery. The handful of us who went on with the qualitative process began to sit on the same side of the room talking among ourselves and feeling very engaged in the process. Other classmates were frustrated.

This cadre of students went on and were clear after just one semester that qualitative research met our needs. We were then together in the year long qualitative strand taught by Bob Bogdan. For the most part, I remember most of us really looking forward to the course. It was a world of ideas. Bob pushed us to question and, without giving in-depth feedback, would ask questions that forced us to re-conceptualize and inquire in a variety of ways. The joy of inquiry is consistent in the experience of qualitative researchers.

Long Apprenticeships

Students of Strauss, Schaztman, and Glaser often struggled with learning grounded theory analysis (Schatzman, 1991), and my experience suggests that other forms of qualitative research are equally challenging to learn. Schatzman wrote that grounded theory analysis does not have a clearly recognizable "research paradigm" and does not portray "how the operations [of grounded theory analysis] link together concretely as a system" (p. 306). Though the writings of Schatzman, Strauss, and Corbin have sought to redress this situation, the challenges of learning and doing exemplary qualitative research may be enduring because of its very nature. Corbin (1991) tells a story about Strauss that illustrates the difficulty of learning and doing qualitative data analysis: during the mid to late 1940s Strauss left qualitative data from two studies analyzed "because he did not really know how to analyze them" (pp. 24-25). LePlay, as discussed earlier, struggled to learn to manage and analyze his data.

As primarily inductive in their approaches, the procedures of almost all qualitative research require that researchers set aside their own theories as much as possible and open themselves to the perspectives of the persons in the situations in which they are conducting their research. Even when using procedures that use pre-established codes and sensitizing concepts, or in forms of analytic induction, researchers put aside pre-formulations in an attempt to understand informants and their situations. Such pre-formulations do not stymie emergence; sometimes they are of great help in aiding researchers in understanding what informants are saying (Gilgun, 1995b) or in sensitizing them to the theoretical implications of their data (Glaser, 1978). Like Glaser, Schatzman (1991) observed that students commonly tended to prematurely bring closure to the analysis by the imposition of "received theory" or they would impose the "received method" of grounded theory analysis before they had carefully analyzed the dimensions of their own data (Schatzman, 1991 pp. 304-305).

Once students trained through seminars graduate and go on to their own professorships, they can become isolated. For example, Marianne McCarthy studied extensively with Strauss and she and several other students did a group independent study over several quarters with Schatzman to analyze their data for their dissertation research. "The group independent study was wonderful," she said in an interview I did with her. "We worked as a group, critiqued each others' fieldnotes and each others memos" (Gilgun, 1993a, p. 6). When she completed her dissertation and left San Francisco to become a professor, she found herself searching unsuccessfully for another group with whom to do analysis. "Doing analysis is an interactional process," she said, "and I didn't have anyone to interact with" (p. 6).

Who Constructs Findings

The isolation that many qualitatively-oriented scholars experience is an additional issue in the on-going development of skills. Analysis is complex and often requires long discussions with other researchers, a process that the seminars heed. Yet, qualitative researchers frequently have few if any like-minded scholars with whom to analyze data. Funding is important in the building of such groups, but funding remains problematic for most qualitative researchers. Many researchers work closely with graduate students on projects, so that at least there is a group of two involved in the analysis. My work has benefitted from interaction with a series of research assistants, who have helped me in my formulation of ideas as I work with data. I've also found paper presentations to be important in fostering my understandings, and I seek opportunities to do presentations and workshops to professional colleagues in the human services. Correspondence through e-mail has linked me more closely with other qualitative researchers. I also teach courses in which I can present my developing ideas. Finally, I convene a qualitative research interest group composed of graduate students and professors that meet regularly to discuss our research. I incorporate feedback from these venues into my analysis.

Group analysis of data, however, might not suit every situation. Some researchers, for example, find spending time alone to work with and think about their data is an important part of their analytic process. The act of writing helps in the clarification and delineation of ideas. Doing the analysis with others who have not been in the field and who are not able to connect with field workers' experiences, especially if there are status and power differences, can be counterproductive. For group analysis to be generative, there appears to be a requirement that the perspectives of the group members be compatible and complementary.

Informants can facilitate data analysis. Barry (1996) developed a continuum of collaboration, from the more "soloist" to the more "coproduced" research (p. 421). In my own long-term research on how persons overcome childhood adversities (Gilgun, 1990a, 1991, 1996 a &

71

b, in press), which involves multiple interviews, I gradually share with informants my understandings of their lives in order to check whether or not I am in tune with their own meanings. Often I am not, and my informants then add nuances to their perspectives that I had not previously been able to grasp. Before submitting articles for publication, I usually share them with one or more informants, again to test whether I am close to their meanings. Other researchers, such as Bloom (1966), provide transcripts of interview to informants. Bloom based her decision on Harding's (1987) idea that an important contribution of feminist research is that it responds to questions women have about their own lives. In some instances, she found, as I did, that such sharing stimulated deeper reflection into personal experience.

The doing of qualitative research, then, ideally involves collaborative work. As researchers conduct their analyses, they may use computer programs to help in data management and to support processes of theorizing and discovery (Richards & Richards, 1994). Researchers also may develop lists, tables, matrices, diagrams such as those described in Miles and Huberman (1994) as they work with data. This level of data analysis is guided by ideas. Thus, the basic skills in qualitative analysis center around interpreting the meanings of the data, not in the technicalities of data management.

Ethics and Emotional Impact

Under ideal conditions, students learning to do qualitative research are well-prepared to deal with the multiple possible happenstances that characterize fieldwork. Although beginners can, without much harm to themselves and others, do informal observations, library research, and simple brief interviews on non-controversial topics, fieldwork is potentially full of risks. Simple and well-supervised tasks probably are sufficient for getting started. Many qualitative studies involve in-depth investigations into sensitive topics. Under these conditions, students require a great deal of supervision in handling their own responses to field work and in interpreting the responses of others. Inexperienced researchers who stride confidently into field settings can, as Punch (1994) noted, be unprepared for the ethical and political dilemmas inherent in field work and may cause a great deal of damage to themselves and to others.

Ethical considerations, then, are yet other reasons to view the learning of qualitative methods as on-going processes that require frequent meeting with others in order to process the gamut of field experiences, including the analysis and interpretation of informants' data and not excluding informants' subjective responses and concerns about field relations.

The development of research teams composed of experienced qualitative researchers and students is an alternative to the seminar format when such seminars are not available and a supplement when they are. Through such teams, students may process a range of responses and interpretations of their field experiences and the more experienced researchers can also model ways of doing so. The research team discussed in Hall and Zvonkovic (1996) is an example of this style of apprenticeship in research on marriage. Other family researchers (e.g., Gilbert, 1996; Kitson et al, 1996) have developed methods of acknowledging and processing emotional aspects of doing qualitative research. Brown (1996) uses a range of approaches to prepare researchers for the subjective dimensions of fieldwork, including using students' research journals in class discussions and role playing being informants and researchers. It is important to note that Brown, like many other methodologists, views education about the uses of subjectivity in research as an acknowledgement of the interconnections of the affective and cognitive domains.

Paying careful attention to the emotional responses of informants, as well as the intellectual content of their words, is an ethical and humane stance that requires the attention of both students and experienced researchers. Informing respondents of the pitfalls and opportunities of participating in the research, stating that respondents are free not to respond, and checking in to see how informants are doing are ways of dealing with informants' emotions (Gilgun, 1994c; Kitson et al, 1996). Such sensitivity to informants requires a great deal of awareness that experienced and new researchers best cultivate in group analysis of field experiences.

Funding and Getting Published

Funding is an issue for qualitative researchers. Though the situation may change in the future, far too often proposals based on qualitative approaches are not funded because they are judged by criteria developed for the evaluation of quantitative work. As discussed earlier, most quantitative work roughly can be categorized as positivistic and Cartesian while most qualitative work is interpretive and often phenomenological. Qualitative work centers around meanings in a variety of situations from a variety of perspectives. The focus in quantitative work, then, is epistemological, while much qualitative work is ontologically-oriented. These two foci are not the same. To judge one by the procedures of the other makes little sense. Much has been written about how to write proposals for funding qualitative research (Marshall & Rossman, 1995; Morse, 1991; 1994). Hopefully within a few years there will be a wide-spread acceptance of methodological pluralism.

From that will come an understanding of the wisdom of funding a range of types of research. Science can be done under a variety of kinds of methods, methodologies, epistemologies, and ontologies.

Guidelines for Evaluation

By now I hope it is clear that there is no one way to do qualitative research. The very richness of these possibilities, however, can render evaluation of qualitative research problematic. Many persons have written about judging quality (cf., among others, Altheide & Johnson, 1994; Ambert et al, 1995; Gilgun, 1993b; Lincoln, 1995, Reason & Rowan, 1981; Smith, 1993; Schwandt, 1996; van Maanen, 1988). From the point of view of common sense, a research report perhaps could best be evaluated in terms of what it purports to be (Gilgun, 1993b). After all, we judge apples by their appleness and oranges by their orangeness. We do not fault an apple because it is not an orange. For example, a report that considers itself phenomenological should present results that represent informants' lived experience. If such a report does not, then it should be revised until the purpose and the intellectual context of the research line up with findings. If authors state their research is based on grounded theory or analytic induction, then the finding must contain a theory. In the case of analytic induction, an initial hypothesis also must be present. If a report states that it is experimental and is pushing the boundaries, say of ethnography to create, perhaps, a personal ethnography, then this report can be evaluated as to whether or not cultural themes and practices are part of the report as well as whether the report is a narrative about the personal meanings of the author.

To facilitate evaluation of qualitative pieces, authors routinely, but not always, state the type of research they are doing and provide citations. Reviewers not familiar with the style of qualitative research can use the references to educate themselves or send the article back to the journal editor who would find a more knowledgeable reviewer. Some articles using qualitative methods do not state the type of research they are doing. As a reviewer, I would fault the authors and ask them to situate themselves in a research tradition. In some experimental work, the tradition may be identified in the article's abstract, but it is there somewhere, if for no other reason than to orient those not familiar with that style of research.

Besides these general guidelines, the views of Glaser and Strauss (1967) and Glaser (1978) continue to be relevant: "grab", modifiability to fit particular situations, an account of procedures that led to the results, and the situating of findings within social science traditions. The idea of on-going emergence implies the idea that there always is more to learn about the phenomena; thus, Glaser and Strauss--and the Chicago School

74

of Sociology tradition on which they have built--have modest goals for the universality of findings. Perhaps because they were concerned that methods and the findings could be misunderstood they also recommended that researchers present their theoretical frameworks in conventional social science language. Using language familiar to audiences of interest to describe methods and findings helps to bridge research traditions.

Depending upon the type of research, many of the desirable qualities Lincoln (1995) identified may be relevant: researchers being clear about their own stances regarding their topics; findings that are relevant not only to other researchers and policy makers but also to communities that have a stake in findings; attention to voice so that multiple points of views--or voices--are represented in research reports, not simply those who have traditionally spoken for others; and accounts of reflexivity that show a deep understanding of the positions of others while staying in touch with one's own experiences, including any transformation that researchers may experience as a result of the research. This long and incomplete list is suggestive; some and not all of these desired qualities are relevant to any particular research report. I think most qualitative researchers would agree on the overall importance of presenting evidence of researchers' immersion in the field, conveyed through rich and deep descriptions that evoke new understandings.

Though researchers from within an interpretive tradition would accept the above qualities as desirable, there are some who consider themselves qualitative researchers who would not. As one example, Clavarino, Najman, & Silverman, (1995), concerned with the ambiguity of analysis, argued forcefully that inter-rater reliabilities must be established in the analysis of qualitative data. They urged other researchers to resist "methodological anarchy" (p. 224). They don't specify what constitutes this "anarchy," but it could be such tradition-bound procedures as group analysis of data that does not involve mathematical inter-rater reliability. Miles and Huberman (1994) also recommend doing inter-rater reliabilities. They use the term *check coding*. They note as a issue in this regard that persons from one social science tradition may not see the same things in data as persons from others. Their discussion suggests that the coders should ultimately agree on the names of the codes and the meanings of the data. Such a stance could be consistent with some philosophies of science, but a viable alternative is to code the same chunk of data in more than one way and to heed the idea that multiple interpretations possible are not only possible but are desirable.

Not all qualitative data must be subjected to inter-rater reliability studies. By the time well-done qualitative research is presented in a research report, researchers and their co-researchers with whom they have analyzed data are so immersed in the data that not only is the analogue of inter-rater reliability already present, but there is a depth and breadth made possible through prolonged discussion and reflection that goes far beyond what highly focused inter-rater reliability studies can offer. Similarly, no one of any of the above described desirable qualities must be in any one study. The paradigm underlying the research guides in making decisions about procedures and interpretive processes. To insist that all qualitative studies must do a quantified assessment of inter-rater reliability or must use other procedures that are inconsistent with the research paradigm would be akin to insisting that the only good apples are those whose juice tastes like the liquid that comes from oranges.

Qualitative interview data are sometimes subjected to inter-rater reliability studies, as Mendenhall, Grotevant, & McRoy (1996) did in their study of couples' movement and non-movement to openness in adoption. They were interested in relatively focused phenomena, and the use of inter-rater reliabilities in the context of their research goals made sense. Given the methodological sophistication that is emerging in these postmodern times, the perspective that one set of criteria fits all research is not operative. Each type of qualitative research productively can be evaluated in terms of what it purports to be doing.

Some qualities are desirable regardless of the paradigms in which they are embedded. Coherent organization of ideas, ideas supported by data, and clarity in the presentation of ideas are some of them. Sussman (1993) identified "heart" as an important quality in any kind of research By heart, he meant a sense that the authors conveyed something meaningful and in which they believe.

Summary

In our own time, the array of possibilities for the design of research points to a methodologically pluralistic future for research on families. More than two decades ago, Glaser (1978) stated that grounded theory is only one of many styles of sociological research and that the field needs *all* perspectives (p. 3, emphasis in the text). Today, there is much more of an intellectual foundation for the pluralism that Glaser made a case for. For many family scholars, the future is exciting because of these possibilities.

There still is limited opportunity for in-depth training in the doing of qualitative research, despite the plethora of research approaches now available in these postmodern times. Learning to do qualitative research requires a long apprenticeship. The philosophical underpinnings of qualitative methods are challenging and quite different from how most of today's researchers have been trained. Qualitative research may most effectively be done in teams, where more than one person becomes deeply immersed in data and therefore can contribute to interpretation. Variety and challenge characterize contemporary qualitative family research. Some researchers learn on their own by trial and error and produce exemplary qualitative research. Others are doing the best they can, but struggle to reach the level of skill required for publication. Once researchers have attained some facility in the doing of qualitative research, finding colleagues with whom to analyze data can be problematic. Processing of field experiences is most effectively done in interaction with others. Technical skills are important, but working with ideas is foundational to qualitative analysis.

The range of types of qualitative research has expanded in contemporary times. Researchers can do tightly controlled qualitative studies that carry on a positivistic tradition or they can attempt to actualize the challenges of postmodernist thinking, as many working within cultural studies are doing. Some approaches are more explicitly emancipatory than others. Some are emancipatory in terms of changing social structures, while others, such as family therapy, focus on interpersonal change. Procedures of induction characterize contemporary approaches, although by now I hope it is clear that deduction and induction are probably present is all research. In qualitative research, however, the emphasis is on induction. Reflexivity, too, is an issue within qualitative family research, with a range of emphases, and with an open field in terms of how subjectivity can be represented in our research. Contemporary qualitative research not only is caught up in postmodern methodological transformations we are now undergoing, but the history of qualitative research shows that today's methodological concerns have roots in the origins of qualitative research and social research in general.

Discussion

Social research originated with qualitative family research. From the beginning, qualitative researchers immersed themselves in the worlds they studied, used inductive methods to study social problem in need of amelioration, and recognized the importance of their own subjectivities and the subjectivities of those being researched. Their methods were pluralistic. In tune with pragmatist views, they used whichever methods fit their research goals: participant observation, interviewing, document analysis, surveys, and use of demographic data. Philosophically, their methods were based on the notions of lived
experience and *verstehen*, or understanding situated in social, cultural, and historical context, in contrast to Cartesian emphases on explanation, objectivity, and mathematics (Hamilton, 1994).

During the recent past, few scholars were aware of the possibilities represented in inductive, experiential, reflexive, and emancipatory research. From about the 1940s to the late 1980s and beyond, Cartesian philosophies eclipsed the human sciences approaches characteristic of the Chicago School of Sociology. When contemporary scholars brought attention back to human experience and understanding as important in social research, the response was immediate and wide-spread. Countless graduate students began pursuing qualitatively-based research for their dissertations. Editors began searching for qualitative family research to place in their journals. There was an outpouring of books that support the development of qualitative methods. Graduate training is becoming more available.

Family scholars are ready to claim their heritage. As we learn more about the traditions in which such research is situated, we can gain confidence in our approaches because we are learning that we have a galaxy of scholars who prepared the philosophical and methodological bases for our work today. Research that is inductive, focuses on human experience, that recognizes researchers' subjectivities, and that is emancipatory is solidly within a long tradition. Feminist perspectives, too, are part of this heritage. The work of Jane Addams and her colleagues at Hull House influenced the intellectual milieu of the Chicago School of Sociology.

How we conduct our research today and the philosophical assumptions that we make are not identical with those of our forbears. On the other hand, many of the ideas of the nineteenth and early part of the twentieth century that undergirded early family research are the ideas that are influencing us today. Glaser's words (1978) on the need for all perspectives are becoming self-evident in contemporary family scholarship and in the social and human sciences in general.

References

Abbott, E. (1910). *Women in industry.* New York: Appleton.

Abbott, E. (1950). Grace Abbott and Hull-House, 1908-1921. Part 1. *Social Service Review, 24,* 374-394.

Abbott, E., & Breckinridge, S. P. (1916). *The Tenements of Chicago, 1908-1935.* Chicago: University of Chicago Press.

Ackerman, N. (1958). *The psychodynamics of family life.* New York: Basic Books.

Adams, B. N. (1988). Fifty years of family research: What does it mean? *Journal of Marriage and the Family, 50,* 5-17.

Alasuutari, P. (1996). Theorizing in qualitative research: A cultural studies perspective. *Qualitative Inquiry, 2,* 371-384.

Allen, K. R. (1994). Feminist reflections on lifelong single women. In Donna L. Sollie & Leigh A. Leslie (Eds.), *Gender, families, and close relationships: Feminist research journeys* (pp. 97-119). Thousand Oaks, CA: Sage.

Allen, K. R. (1989). *Single women/family ties: Life histories of older women.* Newbury Park, CA: Sage.

Allen, K. R., & Pickett, R. S. (1987). Forgotten streams in the family life course: Utilization of qualitative retrospective interviews in the analysis of lifelong single women's family careers. *Journal of Marriage and the Family, 49,* 517-526.

Altheide, D. L., & Johnson, J. M. (1994). Criteria for assessing interpretive validity in qualitative research. In N. K. Denzin & Y. S. Lincoln (Eds.), *Handbook of qualitative research* (485-499). Thousand Oaks, CA: Sage.

Ambert, A. M., Adler, P. A., Adler, P., & Detzner, D. F. (1995). Understanding and evaluating qualitative research. *Journal of Marriage and the Family, 57,* 879-893.

Anderson, N. (1925). *The hobo.* Chicago: University of Chicago Press.

Anderson, N. (1983). A stranger at the gate; Reflections on the Chicago School of Sociology. *Urban Life, 11,* 396-406.

Angell, R. C. (1936). *The family encounters the depression.* New York: Scribner.

Atkinson, P. A. (1988). Ethnomethodology: A critical review. *Annual Review of Sociology, 14,* 441-465.

Baber, K. M., & Allen, K. R. (1992). *Women and families: Feminist reconstructions.* New York: Guilford.

Bailey, K. D. (1984). On integrating theory and method. *Current Perspectives in Social Theory, 6,* 21-44.

Barry, D. (1996). Artful inquiry: A symbolic constructivist approach to social science research. *Qualitative Inquiry, 2,* 411-438.

Barry, K. (1979). *Female sexual slavery.* Englewood Cliffs, N.J.: Prentice-Hall.

Barthes, R. (1974). *S/Z: An essay.* (R. Miller, Trans.). New York: Hill and Wang. Original edition published in 1970 by Editions du Seuil, Paris.

Barton, A. H. (1971). Empirical methods and radical sociology: A liberal critique. In J. D. Colfax & J. L. Roach (Eds.), *Radical sociology.* New York: Basic.

Bateson, G. (1972). *Steps to an ecology of mind.* New York: Ballentine.

Becker, H. S. (1953). Becoming a marihuana user. *American Journal of Sociology, 59,* 235-242.

Becker, H. S. (1988). Blumer's conceptual impact. *Symbolic Interaction, 11,* 13-20.

Becker, H. S., Geer, B., & Hughes, E. (1968). *Making the grade.* New York: Wiley.

Becker, H. S., B. Geer, E. Hughes, and A. L. Strauss. (1961). *Boys in white*. Chicago: University of Chicago Press.

Bell-Scott, P., Guy-Sheftall, B., Royster, J. J., Sims-Wood, J., DeCosta-Willis, M., & Fultz, L. (Eds.) (1991). *Double stitch: Black women write about mothers & daughters*. Boston: Beacon.

Benner, P. (Ed.) (1994). *Interpretive phenomenology*. Thousand Oaks, CA: Sage.

Berger, P., & Luckmann, T. (1966). *The social construction of reality*. New York: Doubleday.

Bernard, J. (1981). *The female world*. New York: Free Press.

Bertalanffy, L. von (1968). *General systems theory: Foundations, development, applications*. New York: George Braziller.

Blaisure, K. R., & Allen, K. R. (1995). Feminism and the ideology and practice of marital equality. *Journal of Marriage and the Family, 57*, 5-19.

Bleier, R. (Ed.) (1984). *Science and gender: A critique of biology and its theories on women*. New York: Pergamon.

Bloom, L. R. (1996). Stories of one's own: Nonunitary subjectivity in narrative representation. *Qualitative Inquiry, 2*, 176-197.

Bott, E. (1957). *Family and social network*. New York: Free Press. Second edition published in 1971.

Boss, P. G. (1987). Family stress. In M. B. Sussman & S. K. Steinmetz (Eds), *Handbook of marriage and the family* (pp. 695-723). New York: Plenum.

Boss, P. G. (1988). *Family stress management*. Newbury Park, CA: Sage.

Boss, P. G. (1993). The reconstruction of family life with Alzheimer's disease: Generating theory to lower family stress from ambiguous loss. In P. G. Boss, W. J. Doherty, R. LaRossa, W. R. Schummn, and S. K. Steinmetz (Eds.), *Sourcebook of family theories and methods: A contextual approach* (pp. 163-166). New York: Plenum.

Bossard, J. H. S., & Boll, E. S. (1950). *Ritual in family living*. Philadelphia: University of Pennsylvania Press.

Bowen, M. (1978). *Family therapy in clinical practice*. New York: Jason Aronson.

Blumer, H. (1928). *Method in social psychology*. Ph.D. dissertation, University of Chicago.

Blumer, H. (1939/1969). An appraisal of Thomas and Znaniecki's *The Polish peasant in Europe and America* (pp. 117-126). Originally published in 1939 in *Social Science Council Bulletin, 44, Critiques of research in the social sciences I*, 69-81.

Blumer, H. (1954/1969). What is wrong with social theory? In Herbert Blumer
(1969/1986), *Symbolic interactionism. (pp* (pp. 140-152) Berkeley: University of California Press. Originally published in Vol. XIX in *The American*

Sociological Review.

Blumer, H. (1969/1986). The methodological position of symbolic interactionism. In H. Blumer, *Symbolic interactionism: Perspective and method* (pp. 1-60). Berkeley: University of California Press.

Bochner, A. P., & Ellis, C. (1996). Taking ethnography into the twenty-first century. *Journal of Contemporary Ethnography, 25,* 3-5.

Bogdan, R. C., & Biklen, S. K. (1992). *Qualitative research for education.* Boston: Allyn & Bacon.

Booth, C. (1889). *Life and labour of the people.* Vol. I. London: Macmillan.

Booth, C. (1903). *Life and labour of the people in London.* Final volume. London and New York: Macmillan.

Brown, J. R. (1996). *The I in science: Training to utilize subjectivity in research.* Oslo: Scandinavian University Press.

Brown, P. (1996). Catskill culture: The rise and fall of a Jewish resort area seen through personal narrative and ethnography. *Journal of Contemporary Ethnography, 24,* 83-119.

Bruner, J. (1990). *Acts of meaning.* Cambridge, MA: Harvard University Press.

Bulmer, M. (1984). *The Chicago School of Sociology: Institutionalization, diversity, and the rise of sociological research.* Chicago: University of Chicago Press.

Burgess, E. W. (1926). The family as a unity of interacting personalities. *Family, 7,* 3-9.

Burgess, E. W. (1927). Statistics and case studies as methods of sociological research. *Sociology and Social Research, 12,* 103-120.

Burgess, E. W. (1932). Editor's preface. In E. Franklin Frazier, *The Negro family in Chicago* (pp.ix-xii). Chicago: University of Chicago Press.

Buttny, R. (1990). Blame accounts sequences in therapy: The negotiation of relational meanings. *Semiotica, 78,* 219-248.

Buttny, R. & Jensen, A. D. (1995). Telling problems in an initial family therapy session: The hierarchical organization of problem-talk. In G. H. Morris & R. J. Chenail (Eds.), *The talk of the clinic: Explorations in the analysis of medical and therapeutic discourse* (pp. 19-47). Hillsdale, NJ: Lawrence Erlbaum.

Carmody, C. (1979). Influence of the world's religions on the status of women. In E. C. Snyder (Ed.), *The study of women.* New York: Harper & Row.

Cavan, R. S., & Ranck, K. H. (1936). *The family and the depression: A study of one hundred Chicago families.* Chicago: University of Chicago Press.

Cavan, R. S. (1983). The Chicago School of Sociology, 1918-

1933. *Urban Life, 11,* 407-420.

Charmaz, K.. (1975). The coroners' strategies for announcing death. *Urban Life, 4,* 296-316.

Charmaz, K.. (1990). 'Discovering' chronic illness: Using grounded theory. *Social Science in Medicine, 30,* 1161-1172.

Charmaz, K., & Preissle, J. (1996). New ethnographies: Review Symposium. *Journal of Contemporary Ethnography, 25,* 390-396.

Chenail, R. (1991). *Medical discourse and systemic frames of comprehension.* Norwood, NJ: Ablex.

Chenail, R. J., & Fortugno, L. (1995). Resourceful figures in therapeutic conversations. In G. H. Morris & R. J. Chenail (Eds.), *The talk of the clinic: Explorations in the analysis of medical and therapeutic discourse* (pp. 71-88). Hillsdale, NJ: Erlbaum.

Chenail, R. J., Itkin, P., Bonneau, M., & Andriacchi, C. (1993, October). Managing solutions in divorce mediation: A discourse analysis. Paper presented at the Twenty-first Annual Society of Professionals in Dispute Resolution International Conference, Toronto, Canada.

Chenail, R. J., Douthit, P., Gale, J., Stormberg, J., Morris, G. H., Park, J., Sridaromont, S., Schmer, V. (1990). "It's probably nothing serious, but..." Parents' interpretation of referral to pediatric cardiologists. *Health Communication, 2,* 165-188.

Chesla, C. A. (1994). Parents' caring practices with schizophrenic offspring. In Patricai Benner (Ed.), *Interpretive phenomenology* (pp. 167-183). Thousand Oaks, CA: Sage.

Chesla, C. A. (1995). Hermeneutic phenomenology: An approach to understanding families. *Journal of Family Nursing, 1,* 68-78.

Chesla, C. A. (1996). Early beginnings of the Qualitative Family Research Network: Interview with Ralph LaRossa. *Qualitative Family Research, 10 (1).*3-9.

Chesla, C., Martinson, A. I., & Muswaswes, M. (1995). Continuities and discontinuities in family relations with Alzheimer's patients. *Family Relations, 43,* 3-14.

Chodorow, N. (1978). *The reproduction of mothering: Psychoanalysis and the sociology of gender.* Berkeley, CA: University of California Press.

Clavarino, A. M., Najman, J. M., & Silverman, D. (1995) The quality of qualitative data: Two strategies for analyzing medical interviews. *Qualitative Inquiry, 1,* 223-242.

Clifford, J. & Marcus, G. E. (Eds.). (1986). *Writing culture: The poetics and politics of ethnography.* Berkeley: University of California Press.

Cohler, B. J. (1988). The human studies and the life history: The Social Service Review Lecture, *Social Service Review, 62,* 552-577.

Comstock, D. E. (1982). A method for critical research. In E. Bredo & W. Feinberg (Eds.), *Knowledge and values in social and educational research* (pp. 370-390). Philadelphia: Temple University Press.

Cook, T. D., & Campbell, D. T. (1979). *Quasi-experimentation: Design and analysis for field settings.* Boston: Houghton Mifflin.

Cooley, C. H. (1930). *Sociological theory and social research.* New York: Holt.

Corbin, J. (1991). Anselm Strauss: An intellectual biography. In D. R. Maines (Ed.). *Social organization and social process: Essays in honor of Anselm Strauss* (pp. 17-42). New York: Aldine de Gruyter.

Cressey, D. (1953). *Other people's money.* Glencoe, IL: Free Press.

Curry, C. (1996). *Silver rights.* New York: Algonquin.

Daly, K. (1995, November). How persons generate theory: Second order stories. Paper presented at the Symposium on Interpreting Qualitative Data, Annual Conference, National Council on Family Relations, November 15-18. 1995.

Deegan, M. J. (1990). *Jane Addams and the men of the Chicago School, 1892-1918.* New Brunswick, N. J.: Transaction.

Demos, V. (1990). Black family studies in the Journal of Marriage and the Family and the issue of distortion: A trend analysis. *Journal of Marriage and the Family, 52,* 603-612.

Denzin, N. K. (1989). *Interpretative interactionism.* Newbury Park, CA: Sage.

Denzin, N. K. (1995). On the shoulders of Anselm. *Mind, Culture, and Activity, 2,* 39-47.

Denzin, N. K., & Lincoln, Y. S. (Eds.) (1994). *Handbook of qualitative research.* Thousand Oaks, CA: Sage.

Dienhart, A. (in press). *Men and women co-constructing fatherhood through shared parenting: Beyond the dominant discourse.* Thousand Oaks, CA: Sage.

Dilthey, W. (1976). *Selected writings* (H. P. Rickman, Ed. & Trans.) Cambridge: Cambridge University Press.

Dobash, E. E., & Dobash, R. P. (1979). *Violence against wives: A case against the patriarchy.* New York: Free Press.

Dollard, J. (1937). *Caste and class in a southern town.* New Haven, CT: Yale University Press.

Dreyfus, H. L. (1991). *Being in the world: A commentary on Heidegger's Being and Time, Division I.* Cambridge, MA: MIT Press.

Durkheim, Emile (1966). *Rules of sociological method.* (Sara A. Soloway & John H. Mueller, Trans.) George E. Catlin, editor. Glencoe: Free Press.

Eichler, M. (1981). Monolithic model of the family. *The Canadian Journal of Sociology, 6,* 367-388.

Ellis, C. (1995). *Final negotiations: A story of love, loss, and chronic illness.* Philadelphia: Temple University Press.

Ellis, C. (1995). The other side of the fence: Seeing black and white in a small southern town. *Qualitative Inquiry, 1,* 147-167.

Fagerhaugh, S. (1975). Getting around with emphysema. In Anselm L. Strauss (Ed.), *Chronic illness and the quality of life* (pp. 99-197). St. Louis: Mosby.

Faris, R. E. L. (1967). *Chicago Sociology 1920-1932.* Chicago: University of Chicago Press.

Farnsworth, E. B. (1996). Reflexivity and qualitative family research: An insider's perspectives in bereaving the loss of a child. In J. F. Gilgun & M. B. Sussman (Eds.) *The methods and methodologies of qualitative family research* (pp. 399-415). New York: Haworth.

Faust, D. G. (1996). *Mothers of invention: Women of the slaveholding south in the American civil war.* Chapel Hill: University of North Carolina Press.

Fine, M. (1988). Sexuality, schooling, and adolescent females: The missing discourse of desire. *Harvard Educational Review, 58,* 29-53.

Fine, M. (1994). Working the hyphens: Reinventing self and other in qualitative research. In N. K. Denzin & Y. S. Lincoln (Eds.), *Handbook of qualitative research* (pp. 70-82). Thousand Oaks, CA: Sage.

Fine, M. (1992). *Disruptive voices: The possibilities of feminist research.* Ann Arbor: The University of Michigan Press.

Fiske, J. (1994). Audiencing: Cultural practice and cultural studies. In N. K. Denzin & Y. S. Lincoln (Eds.), *Handbook of qualitative research* (pp. 189-198). Thousand Oaks, CA: Sage.

Form, W. (1987). Two issues: Documentation and nonstatistical manuscripts. *American Sociological Review, 52,* vi.

Franklin, C. (1995). Expanding the vision of the social constructionist debates: Creating relevance for practitioners. *Families in Society, 76,* 395-407.

Franklin, C. (1996a). Solution-focused therapy: A marital case study using recursive dialectic analysis. *Journal of Family Psychotherapy, 7(1),* 31-51.

Franklin, C. (1996b). Learning to teach qualitative research: Reflections of a quantitative research. In J. F. Gilgun & M. B. Sussman (Eds.). *The methods and methodologies of qualitative family research* (pp. 241-274). New York: Haworth.

Fravel, D. L., & Boss, P. G. (1992). An in-depth interview with the parents of missing children. In J. F. Gilgun, K. Daly, and G. Handel (Eds.), *Qualitative methods in family research* (pp. 126-145). Newbury Park, CA: Sage.

Frazier, E. F. (1932). *The Negro family in Chicago.* Chicago: University of Chicago Press.

Frazier, E. F. (1939). *The Negro family in the United States.* Chicago: University of Chicago Press.

Freedman, J., & Combs, G. (1996). *Narrative therapy: The social construction of preferred realities.* New York: Norton.

Gale, J. E. (1991). *Conversation analysis of therapeutic discourse.* Hillsdale, NJ: Erlbaum.

Gale, J., & Newfield, N. (1992). A conversation analysis of a solution-focused marital therapy session. *Journal of Marital and Family Therapy, 18,* 153-165.

Gale, J. (1996). Conversation analysis: Studying the construction of therapeutic realities. In D. H. Sprenkle & S. M. Moon (Eds.). *Research methods in family therapy* (pp. 107-124). New York: Guilford.

Garfinkel, H. (1967). *Studies in ethnomethodology.* Englewood Cliffs, NJ: Prentice Hall.

Gelles, R. J. (1974). *The violent home: A study of physical aggression between husbands and wives.* Beverly Hills, CA: Sage.

Giddens, A. (1971). *Capitalism and modern social theory.* Cambridge, UK: Cambridge University Press.

Gilbert, K.(1996, July). Collateral damage? Indirect exposure to emotions among students and staff. Paper presented at Essex '96, the Fourth International Social Science Methodology Conference, University of Essex, July 1-5.

Gilgun, Jane F. (1990a). The sexual development of men sexually abused as children. In Mic Hunter (Ed.), *The sexually abused male: Prevalence, impact, and treatment* (pp. 177-190). Lexington, MA: Lexington Books.

Gilgun, J. F. (1990, November). The Place of Qualitative Methods in the Study of the Family, a paper presented on the Pre-Conference Workshop on Theory Construction
and Research Methodology, National Council on Family Relations Annual Meeting, Seattle, WA, November 9-11.

Gilgun, Jane F. (1991). Resilience and the intergenerational transmission of child sexual abuse. In Michael Q. Patton (Ed.), *Family sexual abuse: Frontline research and evaluation* (pp. 93-105). Newbury Park, CA: Sage.

Gilgun, J. F. (1992a, November). Chicago days: Handel, Lopata, and Strauss tell stories of their lives as students at Chicago. *Qualitative Family Research, 6 (2),* 3-6.

Gilgun, Jane F. (1992b). Definitions, methods, and methodologies in qualitative family research. In J. F. Gilgun, K. Daly, and G. Handel (Eds.), *Qualitative methods in family research* (pp. 22-41). Newbury Park, CA: Sage.

Gilgun, J. F. (1992c, May). Field methods training in the Chicago School traditions: The early career of Bob Bogdan. *Qualitative Family Research, 6(1),* 8-11.

Gilgun, J. F. (1992d). Hypothesis generation in social work

research. *Journal of Social Service Research, 15,* 113-135.

Gilgun, J. F. (1993a, November). Dimensional analysis and grounded theory: Interviews with Leonard Schatzman. *Qualitative Family Research, 7(1-2),* 1-2, 4-7.

Gilgun, J. F. (1993b). Publishing research reports based on qualitative methods. *Marriage & Family Review, 18,* 177-180.

Gilgun, J. F. (1994a). A case for case studies in social work research. *Social Work, 39,* 371-380.

Gilgun, J. F. (1994b). Avengers, conquerors, playmates, and lovers: A continuum of roles played by perpetrator of child sexual abuse. *Families in Society, 75,* 467-480.

Gilgun, J. F. (1994c) Freedom of choice and research interviewing in child sexual abuse. In B. G. Compton & B. Galaway, *Social work processes* (5th ed.) (pp. 358-368). Chicago: Dorsey. Also appeared in the 3rd and 4th editions.

Gilgun, J. F. (1994d). Hand into glove: Grounded theory and social work practice research. In William Reid & Edmund Sherman (Eds.), *Qualitative methods and social work practice research* (pp. 115-125). New York: Columbia University Press.

Gilgun, J. F. (1995a, November). "Fingernails Painted Red: A Reflexive, Semiotic Analysis of a Case of Family Murder, " paper presented at the symposium on Interpreting Qualitative Data, at the annual meeting, National Council on Family Relations, Portland, Oregon, November 15-18.

Gilgun, J. F. (1995b). We shared something special: The moral discourse of incest
perpetrators. *Journal of Marriage and the Family, 57,* 265-281.

Gilgun, J. F. (1996a). Human development and adversity in ecological perspective:
Part 1: A conceptual framework. *Families in Society, 77,* 395-402.

Gilgun, J. F. (1996b). Human development and adversity in ecological perspective:
Part 2: Three patterns. *Families in Society, 77, 2,* 459-476.

Gilgun J. F. (in press). Mapping resilience as process among adults with childhood adversities. In H. McCubbin, J. Futrell, and A. Thompson (Eds.), *Resilience in Families: Qualitative Approaches.* Madison, WI: Center for Excellence in Family Studies.

Gilgun, J. F., & Sussman, M. B. (Eds.) (1996). *The methods and methodologies of qualitative family research.* New York: Haworth. Monograph from a special issue of *Marriage & Family Review, 24 (1-4).*

Gilgun, J. F., K. Daly, & G. Handel (Eds.). (1992). *Qualitative methods in family research.* Newbury Park, CA: Sage.

Gilligan, C. (1982). *In a different voice: Psychological theory and women's development*. Cambridge: Harvard University Press.

Gilligan, S., & Price, R. (1993). *Therapeutic conversations*. New York: Norton.

Giorgi, A., Fischer, W. F., & von Eckartsberg, R. (Eds.) (1971). *Duquesne studies in phenomenological psychology* (Vol. 1). Pittsburgh: Duquesne University Press.

Giorgi, A., Fischer, W. F., & Murray, E. (Eds.). (1975), *Duquesne studies in phenomenological psychology* (Vol. 2). Pittsburgh: Duquesne University Press.

Giorgi, A., Knowles, R., & Smith, D. L. (1979). *Duquesne studies in phenomenological psychology* (Vol. 3). Pittsburgh: Duquesne University Press.

Glaser, B. (1978). *Theoretical sensitivity*. Mill Valley, CA: Sociology Press.

Glaser, B. (1992). *Basics of grounded theory analysis*. Mill Valley, CA: Sociology Press.

Glaser, B., & Strauss, A. (1967). *The discovery of grounded theory*. Chicago: Aldine.

Gluckman, M. (1971). Preface. In Elizabeth Bott, *Family and social network* (2nd ed.) (pp. xiii-xxx). New York: Free Press.

Goldstein, H. (1996). *The Home on Gorham Street and the Voices of its Children*. Tuscaloosa, AL: University of Alabama Press.

Gordon, L. (1977). *Women's body, women's right: A social history of birth control in America*. New York: Penguin.

Gubrium, J. F, & Holstein, J. A. (1990). *Where is family?* Mountain View, CA: Mayfield.

Gubrium, J. F., & Holstein, J. A. (1993). Family discourse, organizational embeddedness, and local enactment. *Journal of Family Issues, 14*, 66-81.

Guba, E. (Ed.) (1990). *The paradigm dialogue*. Newbury Park, CA: Sage.

Guba, E. & Lincoln, Y. S. (1994). Competing paradigms in qualitative research. In N. K. Denzin & Y. S. Lincoln (Eds.), *Handbook of qualitative research* (pp. 105-117). Thousand Oaks, CA: Sage.

Gurman, A., Kniskern, D., & Pinsof, W. (1986). Research on the process and outcome of marital and family therapy. In S. Bergin & A. Garfield (Eds.), *Handbook of psychotherapy and behavior change* (3rd ed.) (pp. 565-624). New York: Wiley.

Habermas, J. (1971). *Knowledge and human interests*. (J. J. Shapiro, Trans.). Boston: Beacon.

Haley, J. (1987). *Family problem solving* (2nd ed.). San Francisco: Jossey-Bass.

Hall, L., & Zvonkovic, A. (1996). Egalitarianism and oppression in marriage: The effects of research on researchers. In J. F. Gilgun & M.

B. Sussman (Eds.), *The methods and methodologies of qualitative family research* (pp. 89-104). New York: Haworth.

Hamabata, M. M. (1993). *Crested kimono: Power and love in the Japanese business family.* Ithaca, NY: Cornell University Press.

Hamilton, D. (1994). Traditions, preferences, and postures in applied qualitative research. In N. K. Denzin & Y. S. Lincoln (Eds.), *Handbook of qualitative research* (pp. 60-69). Thousand Oaks, CA: Sage.

Hamilton, G. V. (1929). *A research in marriage.* New York: Albert & Charles Boni.

Hammersley, M. (1989). *The dilemma of qualitative method: Herbert Blumer and the Chicago tradition.* London: Routledge.

Hanawalt, B. (1996). The composite biography as a methodological tool for the study of childhood in history. In J. F. Gilgun & M. B. Sussman (Eds.) *The methods and methodologies of qualitative family research* (pp. 323-334). New York: Haworth.

Hanawalt, B. A. (1993). *Growing up in medieval London.* New York: Oxford University Press.

Hanawalt, B. A. (1986). *The ties that bound: Peasant families in medieval England.* New York: Oxford University Press.

Handel, G. (1965). Psychological study of whole families. *Psychological Bulletin, 63,* 19-41.

Handel, G. (Ed.) (1967). *The psychosocial interior of the family.* Chicago: Aldine.

Handel, G. (Ed.) (1988). *Childhood socialization.* New York: Aldine.

Handel, G. (1991). Case study in family research. In J. R. Geagin, A. M. Orum, & G. Sjoberg (Eds.), *A case for the case study* (pp. 244-268). Chapel Hill: University of North Carolina Press.

Handel, G. (1992). The qualitative tradition in family research. In J. F. Gilgun, K. Daly, and G. Handel (Eds.), *Qualitative methods in family research* (pp. 12-21). Newbury Park, CA: Sage.

Handel, G. (1996). *Family Worlds* and qualitative family research. In J. F. Gilgun & M. B. Sussman (Eds.). *The methods and methodologies of qualitative family research* (pp.335-348). New York: Haworth.

Handel, G., & Whitchurch, G. G. (Eds.) (1993). *The psychosocial interior of the family* (4th ed.) (pp. 69-85). New York: Aldine.

Harding, S. (Ed.). (1987). *Feminism and methodology.* Bloomington: Indiana University Press.

Harding, S. (1991). *Whose science? Whose knowledge? Thinking form women's lives.* Ithaca, N. Y.: Cornell University Press.

Heidegger, M. (1962/1927). *Being and time* (J. Macquarried & E. Robinson, Trans.). New York: Harper & Row. (Original work published in 1927).

Hess, R. D., & Handel, G. (1959). *Family worlds: A psychosocial approach to family life.* Chicago: University of Chicago Press.

Hill, R. (1981). Whither family research in the 1980s: Continuities, emergence, constraints, and new horizons. *Journal of Marriage and the Family, 43,* 255-257.

Hochschild, A. R. (1983). *The managed heart: Commercialization of human feeling.* Berkeley: University of California Press.

Hoffman, L. (1981). *Foundations of family therapy: A conceptual framework for systems change.* New York: Basic.

Holbrook, T. L. (1996). Document analysis: Contrasts between official case records and the journal of a woman on welfare. In J. F. Gilgun & M. B. Sussman (Eds.). *The methods and methodologies of qualitative family research* (pp. 41-56). New York: Haworth.

Holstein, J. A., & Gubrium, J. F. (1994). Phenomenology, ethnomethodology, and interpretive practice. In N. K. Denzin & Y. S. Lincoln (Eds.), *Handbook of qualitative research* (pp. 262-272). Thousand Oaks, CA: Sage.

hooks, b. (1981). *Ain't I a Woman? Black women and feminism.* Boston: South End Press.

hooks, b. (1984). *Feminist theory: From margin to center.* Boston: South End Press.

Hunt, M. (1970). *The affair.* New York: World.

Hodges, H. A. (1994). *William Dilthey: An introduction.* London: Routledge.

Hull-House maps and papers, by residents of Hull-House, a social settlement. A presentation of nationalities and wages in a congested district of Chicago, together with comments and essays on problems growing out of the social conditions. New York: Crowell.

Husserl, E. (1931). *Ideas* (W. R. Boyce Gibson, Trans.) London: Allen & Unwin.

Husserl, E. (1977). *Basic writings* (D. Krell, Ed.). New York: Harper & Row.

Jago, B. J. (1996). Postcards, ghosts, and fathers: Revising family stories. *Qualitative Inquiry, 2,* 495-516.

Janeway, E. (1980). Who is Sylvia? On the loss of sexual paradigms. *Signs, 5,* 573-589.

Jick, T. D. (1979). Mixing qualitative and quantitative methods: Triangulation in action. *Administrative Science Quarterly, 24,* 602-611.

Johnson, C. S. (1922). *The Negro in Chicago: A study of race relations and a race riot.* Chicago: University of Chicago Press.

Kantor, D., & Lehr, W. (1975). *Inside the family: Toward a theory of family process.* New York: Harper & Row.

Keeney, B. P. (1990). *Improvisational therapy.* St. Paul: Systemic Therapy Press.

Keeney, B. P., & Ross, J.M. (1985). *Mind in therapy: Constructing systemic family therapies.* New York: Basic Books.

Keeney, B. P., & Bobele, M. (1989). A brief note on family violence. *Australian and New Zealand Journal of Family Therapy, 10(2),* 93-95.

Kidder, L. H. (1981). Qualitative research and quasi-experimental frameworks.
In M. B. Brewer & B. E. Collins (eds.) *Scientific inquiry and the social sciences.* (pp., 226-256). San Francisco: Jossey-Bass Publishers.

Kitson, G.C., Clark, R. D., Rushforth, N .B., Brinich, P. M., Sudak, H. S., & Zyzanski, J. (1996). Research on difficult family topics: Helping new and experienced   researchers cope with research on loss. *Family Relations, 45,* 183-188.

Komarovsky, M. (1940). *The unemployed man and his family.* New York: Dryden.

Komarovsky, M. (1962). *Blue-collar marriage.* New York: Random House.

Lamendola, F. P., & Margaret A. Newman (1994). The paradox of HIV/AIDS as expanding consciousness. *Advances in Nursing Science, 16 (3),* 13-21.

LaRossa, R. (1983). The transition to parenthood and the social reality of time. *Journal of Marriage and the Family, 45,* 579-589.

LaRossa, R. (1988). Renewing our faith in qualitative family research. *Journal of Contemporary Ethnography, 17,* 243-260.

LaRossa, R., & LaRossa, M. M. (1981). *The transition to parenthood: How infants change families.* Beverly Hills, CA: Sage.

LaRossa, R., & Wolf, J. (1985). On qualitative family research. *Journal of Marriage and the Family, 47,* 531-541.

LaRossa, R. & Reitzes, D. C. (1993). Symbolic Interactionism and Family Studies. In P. G. Boss, W. J. Doherty, R. LaRossa, W. R. Schummn, & S. K. Steinmetz (Eds.), *Sourcebook of family theories and methods: A* contextual approach (pp. 135-163). New York: Plenum.

Larzelere, R. E., & Klein, D. M. (1987). Methodology. In Marvin B. Sussman & Suzanne K. Steinmetz (Eds), *Handbook of marriage and the family* (pp. 125-155). New York: Plenum.

Lasch, C. (1977). *Haven in a heartless world: The family besieged.* New York: Basic.

Lather, P. (1991). *Getting smart: Feminist research and pedagogy with/in the postmodern.* New York: Routledge.

Lavee, Y., & Dollahite, D. C. (1991). The linkage between theory and research in family science. *Journal of Marriage and the Family, 53,* 361-373.

Laws, J. L. (1979). *The second X: Sex role and social role.* New York: Elsevier.

LeCompte, M. D. (1993). A framework for hearing silence: What does telling stories mean when we are supposed to be doing science? In D. McLaughlin & W. G. Tierney (Eds.), *Naming silenced lives: Personal narratives and the process of educational change* (pp. 2-9). New York: Routledge.

LeCompte, M.D. & Goetz, J. P. (1982). Problems of reliability and validity in ethnographic research. *Review of Educational Research, 52*, 31-60.

Leininger, M. (1969). Ethnoscience: A new and promising research approach for the health sciences. *Image, 3 (1)*, 2-8.

Leininger, M. (1978). *Transcultural nursing: Concepts, theories and practices.* New York: Wiley.

Leininger, M. (1985). *Qualitative research methods in nursing.* Orlando, FL: Grune & Stratton.

Leonard, V. W. (1994). In Patricia Benner (Ed.) (1994). *Interpretive phenomenology* (pp. 43-63). Thousand Oaks, CA: Sage.

LePlay, F. (1855). *Les ouvriers europeens.* Tours: Alfred Mame.

LePlay, F. (1879). *Les ouvriers europeens* (2nd ed.) Vol 1. Paris: Alfred Mame et fils.

LePlay, F. E. (1866). *La reforme social en France.* Paris: Dentu.

Lewin, K. (1935). *A dynamic theory of personality.* New York: McGraw Hill.

Lewin, K. (1936). *Principles of topological psychology.* New York: McGraw-Hill.

Lewis, O. (1962). *Five families.* New York: Wiley.

Lewis, O. (1963). *The children of Sanchez.* New York: Vintage.

Lewis, O. (1964). *Pedro Martinez.* New York: Random house.

Lewis, O. (1965). *La Vida.* New York: Vintage.

Lincoln, Y. (1995). Emerging criteria for quality in qualitative and interpretive research. *Qualitative Inquiry, 1*, 275-289.

Lincoln, Y. S., Guba, E. G. (1985). *Naturalistic inquiry.* Newbury Park, CA: Sage.

Lindesmith, A. R. (1947). *Opiate addiction.* Bloomington, IN: Principia.

Lindesmith, A. R., Strauss, A. L., & Denzin, N. K. (1975). *Social psychology* (5th ed.). New York: Holt, Rinehart and Winston.

Lopata, H. Z. (1971). *Occupation: Housewife.* Oxford: Oxford University Press

Lopata, H. Z. (1973). *Widowhood in an American city.* Cambridge, MA: Schenkman.

Lopata, H. Z. (1979). *Women as widows: Support systems.* New York: Elsevier.

Lopata, H. Z. (1984). *City women: Work, jobs, occupations, careers.* Volume 1: *America* (with C. A. Miller & D. Barnewolt).

Lopata, H. Z. (1985). *City women: Work, jobs, occupations, careers.* Volume 2: *Chicago* (with D. Barnewolt & C. A. Miller). New York:

Praeger.

Lopata, H. Z. (1992a). *Circles and settings: Role Changes of American Women*. Philadelphia, Temple University Press.

Lopata, H. Z. (1992b, May). Sensitizing concepts, historical analysis, and role theory. *Qualitative Family Research, 6(1)*, 1-2, 13.

Lopata, H. Z. (1996). *Current widowhood*. Thousand Oaks, CA: Sage.

Lipman-Blumen, J. (1984). *Gender roles and power*. Englewood Cliffs, NJ: Prentice-Hall.

Lofland, J., & Lofland, L. H. (1995). *Analyzing social settings: A guide to qualitative observation and analysis* (3rd ed.). Belmont, CA: Wadsworth.

Lynch, M., & Peyrot, M. (1992). Introduction: A reader's guide to ethnomethodology. *Qualitative sociology, 15*, 113-122.

McCabe, A., & C. Peterson (1991). *Developing narrative structure*. Hillsdale, N.J.: Erlbaum.

McLaughlin, D., & Tierney, W. G. (Eds.) (1993). *Naming silenced lives: Personal narratives and the process of educational change* (pp. 2-9). New York: Routledge.

McCubbin, H., Cauble, E., & Patterson, J. M. (Eds.) (1984). *Family stress, coping and social support*. Springfield, IL: Thomas.

McCubbin, H. I., & Thompson, A. I. (1989). *Balancing work and family life on Wall Street: Stockbrokers and families coping with economic instability*. Edina, MN: Burgess International.

McCubbin, H. I., Thompson, E. A., Thompson, A. I., & Fromer, J. E. (Eds.) (1994). *Sense of Coherence and resiliency: Stress, coping, and health*. Madison, WI: Center for Excellence in Family Studies.

McKinney, J. C. (1966). *Constructive typology and social theory*. New York: Appleton-Century-Crofts.

McMahon, M. (1995). *Engendering motherhood: Identity and transformation in women's lives*. New York: Guilford.

Manning, P. K. (1982). Analytic induction. In R. B. Smith & P. K. Manning (Eds.), *Qualitative methods, Vol. II, of Handbook of Social Sciences* (pp. 273-302). Cambridge, MA: Ballinger.

Manning, P. K., & Cullum-Swan, B. (1994). Narrative, content, and semiotic analysis. In N. K. Denzin & Y. S. Lincoln (Eds.), *Handbook of qualitative research* (pp. 463-477). Thousand Oaks, CA: Sage.

Martin, R. R. (1995). *Oral history in social work: Research, assessment, and intervention*. Thousand Oaks, CA: Sage.

Matthews, F. H. (1977). *Quest for an American sociology: Robert E. Park and the Chicago School*. Montreal: McGill-Queens University Press.

Mendenhall, T. J., Grotevant, H. D., & McRoy, R. G. (1996). Adoptive couples: communication and changes made in openness levels.

Family Relations, 45, 223-229.

Merleau-Ponty, M. (1962). *Phenomenology of perception* (C. Smith, Trans.). London: Routledge & Kegan Paul.

Miles, M. B., & Huberman, A. M. (1994). *Qualitative data analysis* (2nd ed.). Thousand Oaks, CA: Sage.

Minuchin, S. (1974). *Families and family therapy.* Cambridge, MA: Harvard University Press.

Minuchin, S., & Fishman, H. C. (1981). *Family therapy techniques.* Cambridge,   MA: Harvard University Press.

Mischler, E. G. (1990). Validation in inquiry-guided research: The role of exemplars in narrative studies. *Harvard Educational Review, 60,* 415-442).

Moon, S. M., Dillon, D. R., & Sprenkle, D. H. (1990). Family therapy and qualitative research. *Journal of Marital and Family Therapy, 16,* 357-373.

Morgaine, C. A. (1992a). Alternative paradigms in family life education. *Family Relations, 41,* 12-17.

Morgaine, C. A. (1992b). Beyond prevention; A program for empowering parents and professionals. *Family Science Review, 5,* 65-84.

Morgaine, C. A. (1994). Enlightenment for emancipation: A critical theory of self-formation. *Family Relations, 43,* 325-335.

Morris, G. H., & Chenail, R. J. (Eds.). (1995). *The talk of the clinic: Explorations in the analysis of medical and therapeutic discourse* (pp. 19-47). Hillsdale, NJ: Lawrence Erlbaum.

Morrow, R. A., with Brown, D. D. (1994). *Critical theory and methodology.* Thousand Oaks, CA: Sage.

Morse, J. M. (1991). On the evaluation of qualitative proposals. *Qualitative Health Research, 1,* 147-151.

Morse, J. M. (1994). Designing funded qualitative research. In N. K. Denzin & Y. S. Lincoln (Eds.), *Handbook of qualitative research* (pp. 220-235). Thousand Oaks, CA: Sage.

Mowrer, E. R. (1927). *Family disorganization: An introduction to a sociological analysis.* Chicago: University of Chicago Press.

Mowrer, E. R. (1932). *Family.* Chicago: The University of Chicago Press.

Mowrer, E. R. with Harriet R. Mowrer (1928). *Domestic discord: Its analysis and treatment.* Chicago: University of Chicago Press.

Murray, S. B. (1996). "We all love Charles:" Men in child care and the social construction of gender. *Gender & Society, 10,* 368-387.

Marshall, C., & Rossman, G. B. (1995). *Designing qualitative research* (2nd ed.), Newbury Park, CA: Sage.

Mitchell, R. G., Jr., & Kathy Charmaz (1996). Telling tales, writing stories: Postmodernist visions and realist images in ethnographic writing. *Journal of   Contemporary Ethnography, 25,* 144-166.

Moustakas, C. (1994). *Phenomenological research methods*. Thousand Oaks, CA: Sage.

Nadeau, J. (in press). *Families making sense of death: Meaning-making in bereavement*. Thousand Oaks, CA: Sage.

Newfield, N. A., Kuehl, B. P., Joanning, H. P. & Quinn, W. H. (1990). A mini ethnography of the family therapy of adolescent drug abuse: The ambiguous   experience. *Alcoholism Treatment Quarterly, 7,* 57-79.

Newfield, N. A., Joanning, H. P., Kuehl, B. P., Quinn, W. H. (1991). We can tell you about "psychos" and "shrinks": An ethnography of the family therapy of adolescent drug abuse. In T. C. Todd & M. D. Selekman (Eds.), *Family therapy approaches with adolescent substance abuse* (277-310). Boston: Allyn & Bacon.

Newman, M. A. (1986). *Health as expanding consciousness*. St. Louis, MO: Mosby.

Newman, M. A. (1989). The spirit of nursing. *Holistic Nursing Practice, 3 (3),* 1-6.

Newmark, M., & Beels, C. (1994). The misuse and use of science in family therapy. *Family Process, 33,* 3-17.

Nosek, M. A., Young, M. E., Rintala, D. H., Howland, C. A., Foley, C. C., & Bennett J. L. (1995). Barriers to reproductive health maintenance among women with physical disabilities. *Journal of Women's Health, 4,* 505-18.

Noth, W. (1995). *Handbook of semiotics*. Bloomington: Indiana University.

Nye, F. I. (1988). Fifty years of family research, 1937-1987. *Journal of Marriage and the Family, 50,* 305-316.

Oakley, A. (1974). *The sociology of housework*. New York: Pantheon.Source

Olesen M., Heading C., Shadick K. M., & Bistodeau, J. A. (1994). Quality of life in long-stay institutions in England: Nurse and resident perceptions. *Journal of Advanced Nursing, 20,* 23-32.

Olesen, V. (1994). Feminisms and models of qualitative research. In N. K. Denzin & Y. S. Lincoln (Eds.), *Handbook of qualitative research* (pp. 158-174). Thousand Oaks, CA: Sage.

Olesen, V., N. Droes, D. Hatton, N. Chico, & L. Schatzman (1994). Analyzing together: Recollections of a team approach. In A.Bryman & R. G. Burgess (Eds.), *Analyzing qualitative data* (pp. 111-128). London: Routledge.

Olsen, C. S. (1996). African-American adolescent women: Perceptions of gender, race, and class. In J. F. Gilgun & M. B. Sussman (Eds.). *The methods and methodologies of qualitative family research* (105-121). New York: Haworth.

94

Osmond, M. W. (1987). Radical-critical theories. In M. B. Sussman & S. K.Steinmetz (Eds), *Handbook of marriage and the family* (pp. 103-124). New York: Plenum.

Osmond, M. W., & Thorne, B. (1993). Feminist theories: The social construction of gender in families and society. In P. G. Boss, W. J. Doherty, R. LaRossa, W. R. Schummn, and S. K. Steinmetz (Eds.), *Sourcebook of family theories and methods: A contextual approach* (pp. 591-623). New York: Plenum.

Packer, M. (1985). Hermeneutic inquiry in the study of human conduct. *American Psychologist, 40,* 1081-1093).

Packer, M. J., & Addison, R. B. (Eds.) (1989). *Entering the circle: Hermeneutic investigation in psychology.* Albany: State University of New York Press.

Palmer, R. E. (1969). *Hermeneutics: Interpretive theory in Schleiermacher, Dilthey, Heidegger, and Gadamer.* Evanston, IL: Northwestern University Press.

Palmer, V. (1928). *Field methods in sociology.* Chicago: University of Chicago Press.

Patton, M. Q. (1990). *Qualitative evaluation and research methods* (2nd ed.). Newbury Park, CA: Sage.

Park, R. E., & Burgess, E. W. (Eds.) (1921). *Introduction to the science of sociology.* Chicago: University of Chicago Press.

Plager, K. A. (1994). Hermeneutic phenomenology: A methodology for family health and health promotion study in nursing. In Patricia Benner (Ed.), *Interpretive phenomenology* (pp. 65-83). Thousand Oaks, CA: Sage.

Polkinghorne, D. (1983). *Methodology for the human sciences: Systems of inquiry.*
Albany: State University of New York at Albany.

Pollner, M., & McDonald-Wikler, L. (1985). The social construction of unreality: A case study of a family's attribution of competence to a severely retarded child. *Family Process, 28,* 241-254.

Polson, M. & Piercy, F. P. (1993). The impact of training stress on married family therapy trainees and their families: A focus group study. *Journal of Marital and Family Therapy, 4,* 69-92.

Punch, M. (1994). Politics and ethics in qualitative research. In N. K. Denzin & Y. S. Lincoln (Eds.), *Handbook of qualitative research* (pp. 83-97). Thousand Oaks, CA: Sage.

Quint, J. C. (1966). Awareness of death and the nurses' composure. *Nursing Research 15,* 49-55.

Quint, J. C. (1967). *The nurse and the dying patient.* New York: MacMillan.

Rainwater, L., Coleman, R., & Handel, G. (1959). *Workingman's wife*. New York: Oceana.

Rainwater, L. (1970). *Behind ghetto walls*. Chicago: Aldine.

Reason, P., & Rowan, J. (Eds.). (1981). *Human inquiry: A sourcebook of new paradigm inquiry*. New York: Wiley.

Red Collective (1978). *The politics of sexuality in capitalism*. London: Publications Distribution Cooperative.

Reif, L. (1975). Ulcerative colitis: Strategies for managing life. In Anselm Strauss (Ed.), *Chronic illness and the quality of life* (pp. 81-88). St. Louis: Mosby.

Reinharz, S. (1992). *Feminist methods in social research*. New York: Oxford University Press.

Richards, T. J., & Richards, L. (1994). Using computers in qualitative research. In N. K. Denzin & Y. S. Lincoln (Eds.), *Handbook of qualitative research* (pp. 445-462). Thousand Oaks, CA: Sage.

Riessman, C. K. (1990). *Divorce talk: Women and men make sense of personal relationships*. New Brunswick, N. J.: Rutgers University Press.

Riessman, C. K. (1993). *Narrative analysis*. Newbury Park, CA: Sage.

Riessman, C. K. (Ed.). (1994). *Qualitative studies in social work research*. Thousand Oaks, CA: Sage.

Rosenau, P. M. (1992). *Post-modernism and the social sciences*. Princeton, N.J.: Princeton University Press.

Rosenblatt, P. C. (1983). *Bitter, bitter tears: Nineteenth century diarists and twentieth century grief theories*. Minneapolis: University of Minnesota Press.

Rosenblatt, P. C., & Fischer, L. R. (1993). Qualitative family research. In P. G. Boss, W. J. Doherty, R. LaRossa, W. R. Schummn, & S. K. Steinmetz (Eds.), *Sourcebook of family theories and methods: A* contextual approach (pp. 167-177). New York: Plenum.

Rosenwald, G.C., & Ochberg, R. (Eds.). (1992). *Storied lives: The cultural politics of self-understanding*. New Haven, CT: Yale University Press.

Rossi, A., Calderwood, A. (1973). *Academic women on the move*. New York: Russell Sage.

Rubin, J. (1988, January). *Ethics and the concept of the person*. Lecture series at the University of California, San Francisco.

Rubin, L. B. (1976). *Worlds of pain: Life in the working-class family*. New York: Basic Books.

Satir, V. (1967). *Conjoint family therapy*. Palo Alto, CA: Science and Behavior Books.

Schatzman, L. (1991). Dimensional analysis: Notes on an

alternative approach to the grounding of theory in qualitative research. In D. R. Maines (Ed.). *Social organization and social process: Essays in honor of Anselm Strauss* (pp. 303-314). New York: Aldine.

Schatzman, L., & Strauss, A. (1973). *Field research: Strategies for a natural sociology*. Englewood Cliffs, N.J.: Prentice-Hall.

Schwandt, T. A. (1994). Constructivist, interpretivist approaches to human inquiry. In N. K. Denzin & Y. S. Lincoln (Eds.), *Handbook of qualitative research* (pp. 118-137). Thousand Oaks, CA: Sage.

Schwandt, T. A. (1996). Farewell to criteriology. *Qualitative Inquiry, 2*, 58-72.

Schwartz, B. (1994). Where is cultural studies? *Cultural Studies, 8*, 377-393.

Sells, S. P., Smith, T. E., & Sprenkle, D. H. (1995). Integrating qualitative and quantitative research methods: A research model. *Family Process, 34*, 199-218.

Sells, S. P., Smith, T. E., Coe, M. J., Yoshioka, M., & Robbins, J. (1994). An ethnography of couple and therapist experiences in reflecting team practice. *Journal of Marital and Family Therapy, 20(3)*, 247-266.

Selvini-Palazzoli, M., Cecchin, G., Prata, G., & Boscolo, L. (1978). *Paradox and counterparadox*. New York: Aronson.

Shaw, C. (1930). *The jack roller*. Chicago: University of Chicago Press.

Silver, C. B. (1982) (edited, translated and with an introduction by Catherine Bodard Silver. In *Frederic LePlay: On family, work, and social change* (pp. 3-134). Chicago: University of Chicago Press.

Singer, J., & P. Salovey (1993). *The remembered self*. New York: Free press.

Small, A. W. (1916). Fifty years of sociology in the United States, 1865-1915. *American Journal of Sociology, 21*, 712-864.

Smith, K. (1993). *After the demise of empiricism: The problem of judging social and education inquiry*. Norwood, NJ: Ablex.

Smith, S. (1993). Who's talking/Who's talking back? *Signs, 18*, 392-407.

Smith, T. E., Winston, M., & Yoshioka, M. (1992). A qualitative understanding of reflective-teams II: Therapists' perspectives. *Contemporary Family Therapy, 14*, 419-432.

Smith, T.E., Yoshioka, M., & Winston, M. (1993). A qualitative understanding of Reflecting teams I: Clients' perspectives. *Journal of Systemic Therapies, 12*, 29-45.

Smith, T. E., Sells, S. P., & Clevenger, T. (1994). Ethnographic content analysis of couple and therapist perceptions in a reflecting team setting. *Journal of Marital and Family Therapy, 20*, 267-286.

SmithBattle, L. (1993). Mothering in the midst of danger. In S. L.

Feetham, S. B. Meister, J. M. Bell, & C. L. Gilliss (Eds.). *The nursing of families* (pp. 141-166). Newbury Park, CA: Sage.

SmithBattle, L. (1994). Beyond normalizing: The role of narrative in understanding teenage mothers' transition to mothering. In Patricia Benner (Ed.), *Interpretive phenomenology* (pp. 141-166). Thousand Oaks, CA: Sage.

SmithBattle, L. (1995). Teenage mothers' narratives of self: An examination of risking the future. *Advances in Nursing Science, 17,* 22-36.

SmithBattle, L. (1996). Intergenerational ethics of caring for adolescent mothers and their children. *Family Relations,* 45, 56-64.

Spradley, J. (1979). *The ethnographic interview.* New York: Holt, Rinehart & Winston.

Sollie, D. L., & Leslie, L. A. (Eds.) (1994). *Gender, families, and close relationships: Feminist research journeys.* Thousand Oaks, CA: Sage.

Sprenkle, D. H., & Moon, S. M. (Eds.). (1996). *Research methods in family therapy.* New York: Guilford.

Sprey, J. (1982). Editorial comments. *Journal of Marriage and the Family, 44,* 5.

Stack, C. B. (1974). *All our kin: Strategies for survival in a black community.*
New York: Harper.

Stacey, J. (1990). *Brave new families: Stories of domestic upheaval in late twentieth century America.* New York: Basic.

Stake, R. (1995). *The art of case study research.* Thousand Oaks, CA: Sage.

Stamp, G. H. (1991). Family conversation: Description and interpretation. *Family Process, 30,* 251-263.

Stanley, L., & Wise, S. (1983). *Breaking out: Feminist consciousness and feminist research.* London: Routeledge & Kegan Paul.

Steedman, C. (1990). *Childhood, culture and class in Britain: Margaret McMillan, 1860-1931.* New Brunswick, NJ: Rutgers University Press.

Stern, P. N. (1980). Grounded theory methodology: Its uses and processes. *Image, 12,* 29-23.

Stern, P. N. (1985). Using grounded theory method in nursing research. In M. Leininger (Ed.), *Qualitative research methods in nursing* (pp. 149-160). Orlando, FL: Grune & Stratton.

Stivers, C. (1993). Reflections on the role of personal narrative in social science. *Signs, 18,* 408-425)

Strauss, A. (1987). *Qualitative analysis for social scientists.* New York: Cambridge University Press.

Strauss, A., & Corbin, J. (1990). *Basics of qualitative research: Grounded theory procedures and techniques.* Newbury Park, CA: Sage.

Strauss, A., L., & Glaser, B. G. (1970). *Anguish: A case history of a dying trajectory.* Mill Valley, CA: Sociology Press.

Strauss, A., L. Schatzman, R. Bucher, D. Ehrlich, & M. Sabshin (1964). *Psychiatric ideologies and institutions.* New York: Free Press.

Sussman, Marvin B. (1993). Commentary on publishing. *Marriage & Family Review, 18,* 109-117.

Taylor, C. (1985). *Human agency and language: Philosophical papers I.* Cambridge, MA: Cambridge University Press.

Taylor, C. (1989). *Sources of the self: The making of the modern identity.* Cambridge, MA: Harvard University Press.

Taylor, C. (1991). *The ethics of authenticity.* Boston: Harvard University Press.

Thomas, D. L., & Wilcox, J. E. (1987). The rise of family theory: A historical and critical analysis. In M. B. Sussman & S. K. Steinmetz (Eds.), *Handbook of*

marriage and the family (pp. 81-102). New York: Plenum.

Thomas, W. I., & Znaniecki, F. (1918-1920/1927). *The Polish peasant in Europe and America,* Vol. 1-2. New York: Knopf. First published in 1918-1920

Thompson, L. (1992). Feminist methodology for family studies. *Journal of Marriage and the Family, 54,* 3-18.

Thorne, B., with M. Yalom (1982). *Rethinking the family: Some feminist questions.* New York: Longman.

Uttal, L. (1996). Custodial care, surrogate care, and coordinated care: Employed mothers and the meaning of child care. *Gender & Society, 10,* 291-311.

Van Maanen, J. (1988). *Tales of the field: On writing ethnography.* Chicago: University of Chicago Press.

Van Manen, M. (1990). *Researching lived experience: Human science for an action sensitive pedagogy.* Albany: State University of New York.

Vidich, A. J., & Lyman, S. M. (1994). Qualitative methods: Their history in sociology and anthropology. In N. K. Denzin & Y. S. Lincoln (Eds.), *Handbook of qualitative research* (pp. 23-59). Thousand Oaks, CA: Sage.

Visweswaran, K. (1994). *Fictions of feminist ethnography.* Minneapolis: University of Minnesota Press.

Waller, W. (1930). *The old love and the new.* New York: Liveright.

Waller, W. (1934). Insight and the scientific method. *American Journal of Sociology, XL,* 285-297.

Walker, J. A. (1996). Letters in the attic: Private reflections of women, wives, and mothers. In J. F. Gilgun & M. B. Sussman (Eds.), *The methods and methodologies of qualitative family research* (pp. 9-40). New York: Haworth.

Warner, W. L., & Lunt, P. S. (1941). *The social life of a modern community*. Vol. 1 of *The Yankee City Series*. New Haven: Yale University Press.

Wax, R. H. (1971). *Doing fieldwork: Warnings and advice*. Chicago: University of Chicago Press.

Webb, S. &, Webb, B. (1932). *Methods of social study*. London: Longman, Green.

White, M., & Epston, D. (1990). *Narrative means to therapeutic ends*. New York: Norton.

Whyte, W. F. (1943). A slum sex code. *American Journal of Sociology, XLIX*, 24-31.

Wiener, C. L. (1975). The burden of rheumatoid arthritis. In Anselm Strauss (Ed.), *Chronic illness and the quality of life* (pp. 71-80). St. Louis: Mosby.

Wilson, H. A. & Hutchinson, S. A. (1991). Triangulation of qualitative methods: Heideggerian hermeneutics and grounded theory. *Qualitative Health Research, 1*, 263-276.

Wiseman, J. E. (1979). *Stations of the lost: The treatment of Skid Row alcoholics*. Chicago: University of Chicago Press.

Wiseman, J. E. (1981). The family and its researcher in the eighties: Retrenching, renewing, and revitalizing. *Journal of Marriage and the Family, 43*, 263-266.

Wiseman, J. E. (1991). *The other half: Wives of alcoholics and their social-psychological situation*. New York: Aldine.

Wittgenstein, L. (1980). *Remarks on the philosophy of psychology* (2 vols.). Chicago: University of Chicago Press.

Wolcott, H. F. (1994). *Transforming qualitative data: Description, analysis, and interpretation*. Thousand Oaks, CA: Sage.

Wolf, M. (1968). *The house of Lim: A study of a Chinese farm family*. New York: Appleton-Century Crofts.

Wright, M. M. (1995). "I never did any fieldwork, but I milked an awful lot of cows!" Using rural women's experience to reconceptualize models of work. *Gender & Society, 9*, 216-235.

Wuest, J. (1995). Feminist grounded theory: An exploration of the congruency and tensions between two traditions in knowledge discovery. *Qualitative Health Research, 5*, 125-137.

Young, P. V. (1928). The reorganization of Jewish family life in America. *Social Forces, VII*, 238-243.

Young, P. V. (1932). *The Pilgrims of Russian Town*. Chicago: University of Chicago Press.

Zaretsky, E. (1976). *Capitalism, the family, and personal life*. New York: Harper & Row.

Zimmerman, C. C., & Frampton, M. E. (1935). *Family and society: A study of the sociology of reconstruction*. New York: Van Nostrand.

Znaniecki, F. (1934). *The method of sociology*. New York: Farrar &

Rinehart.

Zorbaugh, H. (1929). *The Gold Coast and the slum*. Chicago: University of Chicago Press.

About the Author

Jane F. Gilgun, PhD, LICSW, is a professor, School of Social Work, University of Minnesota, Twin Cities, USA. She does research on the meanings of violence to perpetrators, the development of violent behaviors, and how persons overcome adversities. She has published widely in these areas and on qualitative methods within the Chicago School of Sociology tradition.

She worked at a public Rhode Island child welfare social service agency for several years, returned to graduate school, and then became a professor. She also writes children's books, non-fiction, and articles that are available on Amazon and other internet booksellers. She has many videos on YouTube that include the landscapes in Northwest Ireland, trail riding in Minnesota and elsewhere, horse racing, pig racing, and more.

Her interests include her horses, Padron's Elegante (Ellie) and Finn MacCool, who are mother and son, her dog Jazz, gardening, photography, cooking, the arts, and spending time in County Leitrim and County Sligo, Ireland.

Jane has a bachelor's and master's in English and American poetry from the Catholic University of America and the University of Rhode Island, respectively, a master's in social work from the University of Chicago, a licentiate in family studies and sexuality from the Catholic University of Louvain, Belgium, and a Ph.D. in child and family studies from Syracuse University. She is a licensed independent clinical social worker.